Chapters in Architectural Drawing

Steven H. McNeill
Daniel John Stine

ISBN: 978-1-58503-495-6

T0321009

Examination Copies:

Books received as examination copies are for review purposes only and may not be made available for student use. Resale of examination copies is prohibited.

Electronic Files:

Any electronic files associated with this book are licensed to the original user only. These files may not be transferred to any other party.

SDC
PUBLICATIONS

Schroff Development Corporation

www.schroff.com

Foreword

TO THE STUDENT:

This book has been written with the assumption that the reader has no prior experience hand sketching. Between the graphics and instruction in this book plus the videos (see note on video instruction below), the reader will be able to describe and apply many of the fundamental principles needed to create compelling hand drawings, both freehand and hard lined.

The content of this book is relevant to today's high tech design industry. You will learn what role architectural hand drawing has today compared to cutting edge computer design and rendering software; the two can be leveraged to create crisp, clean sketches with an economy of time! Although you will not be expected to use any software (or electronics) to complete this book, you will be introduced to several methods in which these tools are used. The reader will then be presented with exercises where the "computer" part has already been done so you can focus on the "sketching" part.

Although the book is primarily written with a classroom setting in mind, most individuals will be able to work through it on their own. ENJOY!

Video Instruction:

You will find "video" symbols (example at left) throughout the book. These symbols indicate a short video pertaining to the subject can be found on the DVD. Note the number in the icon and view that video file from the DVD.

TO THE INSTRUCTOR:

As an instructor you are strongly encouraged to request the *Instructors Resource Guide* for this book from the publisher. This guide will provide suggested solutions to exercises, answers to end of chapter questions, as well as lecture suggestions for each chapter. The authors also hope to provide additional exercises via this electronic medium and provide you with any errata information that may arise.

A classroom setting was in the minds of the authors when designing this text. The number of chapters relates closely to the number of weeks in a semester, with each chapter having exercises and questions which can be assigned to the student.

You may contact the publisher with comments or suggestions at:
schroff@schroff.com.

ABOUT THE AUTHORS:

Steven H. McNeill is a registered Architect with 36 years experience in the architectural field. He is the Director of Design at LHB (a 170 person multidiscipline firm; www.LHBcorp.com) in Duluth Minnesota. Mr. McNeill is involved in a broad array of project planning, concept development and design. His skills as a delineator were developed while working for such skilled architects as Duane Thorbeck FAIA and Dennis Grebner FAIA. He is a graduate of the University of Minnesota School of Architecture, has served as President of the American Institute of Architects (AIA) Minnesota, AIA Northern Minnesota, and has been an advisor to the Architecture Department at North Dakota State University (NDSU) and Lake Superior College (LSC) Architectural Technology Program. Steven has arranged sketching presentations for the AIA Minnesota Convention and is a co-founder of the Lake Superior Design Retreat, now in its 21st year (http://www.aia-mn.org/committees/lake_superior_retreat.cfm).

Daniel John Stine is a registered Architect with seventeen years experience in the architectural field. He currently works at LHB (a 170 person multidiscipline firm; www.LHBcorp.com) in Duluth Minnesota as the CAD Administrator providing training, customization and support for two regional offices. Daniel has worked in a total of four firms. While at these firms, he has participated in collaborative projects with several other firms on various projects (including Cesar Pelli, Weber Music Hall – University of Minnesota - Duluth). Mr. Stine is a member of the Construction Specification Institute (CSI) and the Autodesk Developer Network (ADN) and also teaches AutoCAD and Revit Architecture classes at Lake Superior College for the Architectural Technology program; additionally, he is a Certified Construction Document Technician (CDT). Mr. Stine has also written the following CAD/BIM textbooks (also published by SDC Publications):

- RESIDENTIAL DESIGN USING REVIT ARCHITECTURE
- COMMERCIAL DESIGN USING REVIT ARCHITECTURE
- RESIDENTIAL DESIGN USING AUTOCAD
- COMMERCIAL DESIGN USING AUTOCAD

THANKS:

The author's would like to thank their families for the encouragement and support provided during the months leading up to the book's deadline.

The authors would also like to thank their employer, **LHB** (www.LHBcorp.com), for its support of this project, mainly in allowing us to use the office after hours to collaborate and create the videos.

We are grateful to the various individuals who contributed architectural drawings for use in this book so that the reader might gain additional insight (please refer to the Index to find page locations):

- Anderson, Alan
- Booker, Darryl
- Pelli, Cesar
- Poirier, Mark
- Porter, Anne
- Rapson, Ralph (deceased, permission from son Toby Rapson)
- Salmela, David
- Schneuer, Craig
- Thorbeck, Duane

This text has been greatly improved thanks to the following who meticulously reviewed draft manuscripts:

- Anderson, Alan (also for testing with his students)
- Jankofsky, Kurt
- Stine, Cheri

A special thanks to LHB and Amy Rutten and Warren Schulze of Concordia College for allowing us to use sketches, created by McNeill, for the French Language Village.

The videos that accompany this textbook have been created with the wonderful help of Emily McNeill, who shot and edited the videos.

Many thanks go out to Schroff Development Corporation for making this book possible!

Table of Contents

Section One
Introduction + Fundamentals

"An architect's most useful tools are an eraser at the drafting board, and a wrecking bar at the site".
Frank Lloyd Wright 1867-1959

Chapter

1

Introduction

The Architectural drawing process employs both art and science to develop design solutions that are pleasant to look at and withstand the elements --- this textbook will help you develop your sketching abilities while dabbling in real-world architectural techniques.

Hand Sketching in a Digital World

Even with the modern power of the computer and design software the designer must have the ability to sketch by hand and think three-dimensionally.

The very first thoughts of a designer, when working on a new project, involve quickly sketching those thoughts onto paper. The process involves several iterations and overlays before the first line is drawn on a computer. These sketches usually take just a few minutes each and are not typically to scale but are proportionally accurate, something that a good designer has learned to do with practice. These first drawings are not to be presentation quality.

Hand sketching is also useful at client meetings and out **in the field**, where the computer is not always handy or convenient. The architect can sketch possible revisions directly on a set of blueprints, which were printed from computer generated drawings. This represents the best use of time, as all the decision makers are present who would not want to wait for the computer to start up, the project file to load, and the designer to meticulously go through all the steps required by the software to explore various solutions to the problem at hand. Once the meeting is over, the revision sketch can be brought back to the office where the drawings can be updated.

The notion of designing a building is surely exciting and is indeed rewarding. The challenge is to approach the academic process of this career properly and with the right attitude. The would-be designer, even one who can already sketch amazingly well, needs to take "baby steps" and really try to understand the architectural process and building sciences, and develop teamwork and organizational skills to even be moderately good. There are many artists, in the broader sense of the word, who could create an amazing looking architectural sketch which would likely not be buildable, not keep out the rain and wind, not be safe for its occupants, not be sustainable, and not be affordable.

While this text is not meant to teach you all about being a good designer, it is written by two authors with **52 years** of combined architectural experience, who will try to touch on many aspects of the profession in a way that is applicable to the topic at hand throughout this volume. One example might be showing a page directly out of an Architect's sketch book (such as the one below) and talk about the thought process involved in the creation of the page – which may appear random and disorganized.

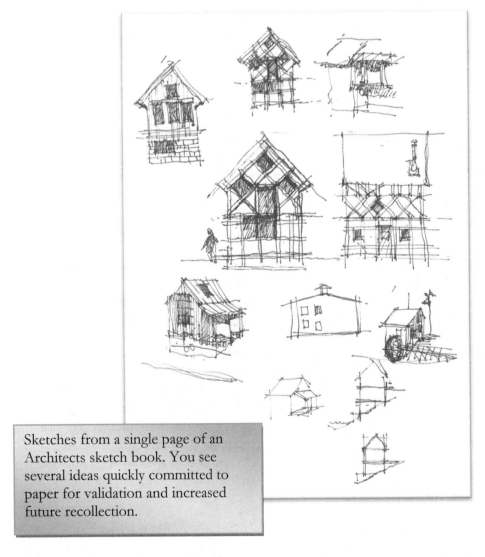

Sketches from a single page of an Architects sketch book. You see several ideas quickly committed to paper for validation and increased future recollection.

"I prefer drawing to talking. Drawing is faster, and leaves less room for lies"
Le Corbusier 1887-1965

What will you learn from this book?

The better question might be how will you learn from this book, rather than what will you learn…

To answer the first question: you will learn the fundamental concepts of freehand sketching architectural drawings. In addition to the fundamentals you will learn many subtle techniques which are covered in a way that is applicable to today's workflow. The basics will be covered thoroughly and start out with simple sketches such as the one below. You will not learn about the larger world of art, but rather will focus on the specific disciple of architecture.

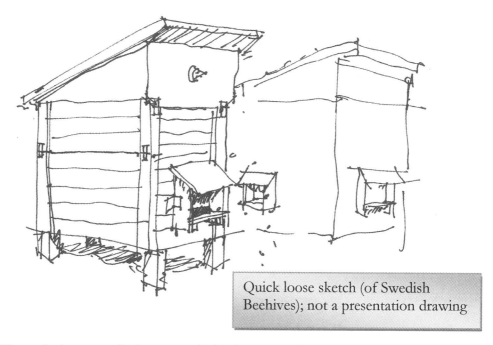

Quick loose sketch (of Swedish Beehives); not a presentation drawing

The techniques studied are cumulative in nature; that is, subsequent lessons build on previous chapters. Following the chapters in order is encouraged by the authors. Quick sketches like the one shown on the next page can be achieved by the reader – it just takes three things:

- A desire to do it
- Patience
- Practice

Now to the question of how you will learn from this textbook: reading and practicing. You must have the desire to read and learn the concepts presented, the time to practice and the patience for results. With these components you should be able to quickly sketch images like the one on the next page without much effort.

You will be presented with many exercises throughout this book. You should plan to complete each of them – this will help to make sure you understand the concepts covered in the chapter and more importantly, give you practice. No one ever became an accomplished artist or designer by just reading. You need to practice, practice, practice! The practice pages in this book are perforated to be torn out and completed on a flat surface. They even have a place for your name and the date so you can hand it in for grading if you are using this book in a classroom setting.

In addition to the reading and exercises, you are also presented with a DVD which contains several videos directly related to the content in the textbook. As mentioned in the preface, the book contains video icons that point you to a specific video on the DVD which relates to information being covered on that page. This is meant to supplement any classroom instruction you have access to and not replace it.

Who knows? You might just become the next great architectural designer! On the other hand, you might find that you are more technically oriented, and that is perfectly fine. Not every architect is a great artist or designer. In fact some architects never draw; they are better managing projects and staff. But even they need to scribble an idea, markup a set of drawings for someone else to revise and understand that a sketch created by a coworker is realistic, buildable and practical. In the end it is your decision to apply yourself and see if you are interested in and capable of this challenge.

What about Computers?

If you are using this book in a classroom setting you may not have chosen to take a sketching class. Hopefully the previous discussion and your successful completion of this textbook will leave you feeling that hand sketching has its place in the digital world. But right now, early in this study, you may be wondering how hand sketching fits in, or blends, with current computer technology. We will quickly consider that question.

First, you should understand that hand sketching and using a computer are both tools in your "toolbox". So, just like carpentry tools, sometimes it's appropriate to use a handsaw while other times you are better off using a power saw. The authors of this book make extensive use of both sets of "tools" in their professional practice and in no way are promoting one over the other; quite the contrary is true, as you will clearly discover later on in the exercises that talk about blending the two techniques for maximum effect and efficiency of time. However, due to limited space and time, the actual use of any particular software will not be covered nor required.

Designers use computers to create incredibly accurate drawings (floor plans, elevations, details, etc.) and, more importantly, drawings which can be modified with ease. Just fifteen years ago most architectural *Construction Drawings* (i.e., drawings used by contractors to construct the building) were still being drawn by hand. Anytime a major change needed to be made, the electric erasers went into full throttle and removed line work from the paper. When finished, the portion of drawing just erased needed to be completely redone – not to mention the layer of eraser shavings that needed to be cleaned from the desk and floor! With computers a major change can be made in just minutes, if not seconds. The drawing below was created in a state-of-the-art Building Information Modeling program called Revit Architecture (by Autodesk). Not only can this program create floor plans and elevations, but it can also create photorealistic renderings with accurate shading based on the location on earth plus month and time of day!

Computer Generated Photorealistic Rending

In addition to software tools used to create construction documents and photorealistic renderings, the designer also has access to programs which can be used earlier in the process for massing (i.e., the main forms of a building) and perspective angle setting. A popular tool enjoyed by many is Google SketchUp, which offers its base software free of charge! (www.google.com/sketchup) This program can be used quickly to refine early design ideas and concepts in a relatively fluid and easy process. The image below is an example of a design created in under an hour using SketchUp.

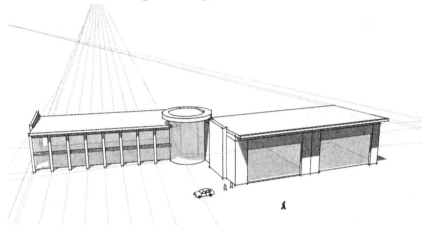

Computer Generated Drawing using Google SketchUp

Finally, there is another set of tools, consisting of software and hardware, which compliment the content of this book quite well. Several software programs exist which allow the designer to hand sketch on the computer screen – allowing one's designs to instantly be digitized and more easily be copied and modified. A few software examples are Adobe Photoshop and Autodesk Sketch Book Pro. Of course, no matter how good your eye-hand coordination is, drawing anything with a big, fat mouse in your hand is not pretty! Thus the hardware part of the equation: a computer screen or laptop on which you can sketch directly, an example of this being depicted to the right.

Even with all these great computer tools you will still need to develop your first ideas by hand sketching (on paper or on-screen). The need to move fast and validate design ideas is important in finding the best solution. One may be able to derive a "good" design solution by trying a handful of options using only a computer, but the "best" solution usually requires many, many more options to be explored, which can be done with an economy of time by hand sketching. Once one or two solutions rise to the top, then the computer is used to further analyze and develop the design – possibly needing to drop back to hand sketching and repeating the process.

Tools of the Trade

For the most part one simply needs paper and a pencil or pen to create a drawing; that is mostly all that is required to progress though this textbook. However, several other tools are often employed by designers, even early on in the design process, which aid in various ways. Here we will take some time to review a few of the most used tools in the designer's toolbox.

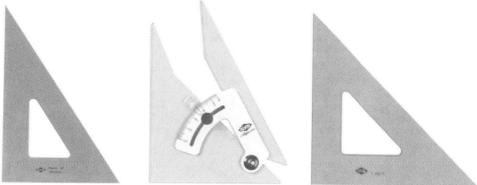

⚓ Triangles are used to create crisp straight lines. The fixed triangle on the left is a 30/60 triangle; which means its sides are 30 degrees, 60 degrees and then 90 degrees. The 30/60 triangle is used for axonometric drawings (as covered later). The adjustable triangle in the middle has a knob that can be loosened in the center which allows the user to swing one half of the triangle to any desired angled and then retighten the knob. The far right triangle is a 45 triangle (i.e. 45,45,90 degrees). Your average architectural illustrator would have one or more of each of these as they come in various sizes and each are useful in different situations; note the large one used in the videos on the DVD. You may think "why not just get the adjustable one", but that is not always convenient when you need to flip it over for example.

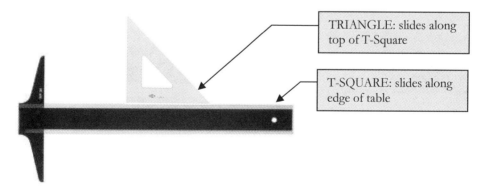

TRIANGLE: slides along top of T-Square

T-SQUARE: slides along edge of table

⚓ T-Squares are not as prevalent these days but still come in handy from time to time. Used in conjunction with the triangles above, you can draw horizontal, vertical and angled lines. The side of the T-Square slides along the edge of a table (which needs to be straight of course). If you have a drafting board, such as the one shown on the next page, you can usually get by without a T-Square.

☉ Rolling Parallel Ruler is a must have for hand sketching. You can line the edge up on the drawing, draw a line along the edge and then move the edge via its tiny wheels that keep the edge parallel with the previous line. This is handy for quickly hatching an area or showing brick on a 2D drawing. However, this would not work for brick in perspective views as the lines need to converge at the vanishing point rather than be parallel (you will learn more about this later on).

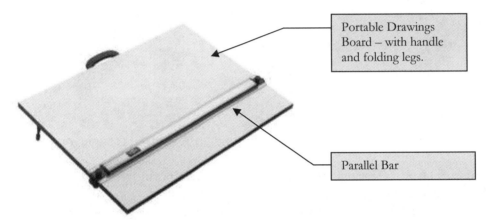

Portable Drawings Board – with handle and folding legs.

Parallel Bar

☉ Drafting Board – portable (shown) or stationary – is a flat drawing surface which is usually angled so the artist has a better view of the drawing surface. The board pictured above includes a parallel bar; which is basically a built-in T-Square guided by the edge of the board and kept parallel by a wire and pulley system under the board. This is not a must for working through this textbook, therefore you can achieve similar results from using a sketch book in the back of a bus!

☉ White Eraser –
Mistakes happen! Avoid the dried out pink erasers on the ends of your pencils.

☉ Dusting Brush – you have to get those eraser crumbs out of the way!

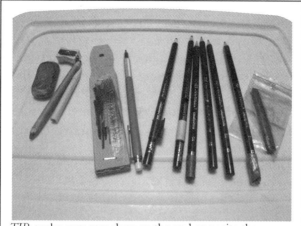

TIP: make sure you sharpen the end opposite the hardness markings so you can tell the pencils apart after they have been sharpened a few times.

The image to the left shows the basic tools required to create a decent architectural freehand sketch. Just about everything shown can be purchased in a "starter kit" at any art supply store or website. The items shown to the left (from left to right) are: Eraser, Sharpener, Blending Sticks, Tip Pointer, Mechanical Pencil, (2) Charcoal Pencils; Soft and Medium, (4) Graphite Pencils; HB, 2B, 4B, and 6B, and a Graphite Stick.

The **ink pens** are great for crisp consistent lines and are used by many designers. However the result is more permanent than pencil. When using special paper (like Mylar) and special erasers you are able to erase the ink line work. The authors of this book recommend you mainly use an ink pen as you learn to sketch so you are not tempted to erase lines; your lines will be bold and more intentional! A felt or gel-type tipped pen is preferred over a ball point pen in most cases.

The **graphite pencils** are often used for architectural freehand sketching. You will typically start with the harder pencils (HB and 2B) and then embellished with the softer, darker pencils (4B and 6B). Pencils provide a nice contrast to the primary line work done with ink pens.

The **tip pointer** is basically several pieces of sandpaper on a stick. This is a convenient place to rub your pencil tip back and forth on to quickly sharpen the tip or create a chisel type tip for special effects.

The **mechanical pencil** can accept "lead" inserts of various types. This tool does not require you to sharpen the pencil and never gets too small to hold.

Prismicolor pencils (or similar brands) in black can be an option for rendering as they do not readily smear.

The **charcoal pencils** are useful for making very heavy black lines on the paper. Charcoal is very soft so the tips need to be sharpened often.

The **blending sticks** are used to smudge the graphite on the paper into a solid gray/black area. A few uses are to create shades and shadows as well as transitions on curved surfaces to name a few.

Sketch Book

The ability to sketch is one that is developed over time and with lots of practice. One way to practice is by using a sketch book. A sketch book can be purchased at any art supply store or website. Sketchbooks come in many shapes and sizes and make sure it is acid free so your sketches will last for many years. With a sketch book and a small sack of pencils, you can practice just about anywhere. Just sitting in the waiting room at the doctor's office, you can practice sketching the space, working on perspective, line weight and detail. Your sketches do not, and should not, always be about architecture. You can practice on anything and everything. One of the examples below is a quick drawing of a BMX bike in action!

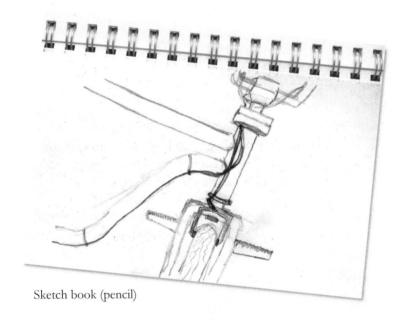

Sketch book (pencil)

Pen & Colored Pencil

Do you have the time?

One of the largest obstacles to becoming a talented artist is time. Like anything in life, you have to spend a certain amount of time honing your skills – be it a sport, an instrument or, in this case, sketching. Try and spend a few minutes each day sketching something, anything. Pay attention to textures, shades and shadows and perspective. Many of us watch a lot of television. Why not have a sketch book nearby and use it during commercials?

The sketch below is an exciting design idea by world famous **Cesar Pelli** of Pelli Clarke Pelli Architects, New Haven, CT. Mr. Pelli has designed many amazing buildings such as the *Petronas Twin Towers* in Kuala Lumpur, Malaysia. This elegant, yet simple, sketch should inspire you as you consider embarking on your study of architectural drawing.

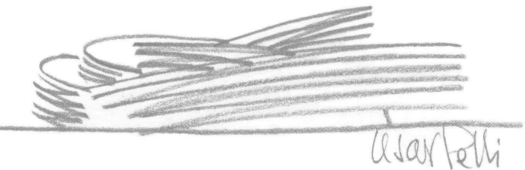

Preliminary sketch of the BOK Center in Tulsa, OK
Image used by permission

Trondheim Cathedral
by **Duane Thorbeck** FAIA

Work or Play?

Everyone should enjoy what they do for a living. Try not to approach sketching from the perspective that you have to do this to get a grade or make lots of money at work. When you focus on doing something with a 110% positive attitude, the grade and money will likely follow. With this attitude you are more likely to retain what you are studying and be prepared to apply it when needed… **so have fun**! You may, in the end, discover sketching is not for you; not all designers are great sketching artists.

N A M E _____   D A T E _____

Self-Exam:
The following questions can be used as a way to check your knowledge of this lesson. The answers can be found at the lower left on this page.

1.   You need to know some design software to use this book. (T/F)

2.   The pink eraser on the end of a pencil is the best to use. (T/F)

3.   Early project drawings should be presentation quality. (T/F)

4.   The _____ triangle can be set to many angles.

5.   You can use a _____ _____ to smudge the graphite on paper.

Review Questions:
The following questions may be assigned by your instructor as a way to assess your knowledge of this section. Your instructor has the answers to the review questions.

1.   Some draw on computers and other by hand, but none do both. (T/F)

2.   Some Architects are better managers than they are designers. (T/F)

3.   The design process involves several iterations and overlays. (T/F)

4.   An HB pencil is harder and darker than a 6B pencil. (T/F)

5.   The DVD is meant to replace classroom instruction. (T/F)

6.   The authors have _____ years combined experience.

7.   _____ is a popular 3D sketching/design software which has a free version.

8.   What does "in the field" mean: _____.

9.   Computers are used to create photorealistic renderings with shadows. (T/F)

10.   A tool used for quickly hatching an area with several parallel lines:

      _____

~blank page~

Views, Scales & Symbols

Every architectural drawing is drawn as if seen from a specific view; these views have specific names which you will learn in this chapter. Also, some architectural drawings are drawn "to scale", which means they are proportional to the real-world intended size of the building. And, just to make sure everyone is on the same page, we will cover some of the various graphics used in architectural floor plans which represent specific parts of a building — e.g., stairs, toilets, kitchen cabinets, etc.

This second chapter will cover some fundamental information which is often relegated to classroom instruction. The authors felt it important to provide this information to ensure later discussions in this manuscript are clearly comprehended, especially for those using this book outside the classroom setting. If the reader is taking a class and the instructor also covers this material, that would be even better!

First you will learn about the various views used to delineate an architectural design, starting with the 2D views and then the various 3D views. The use of line weights to make drawings "read" better is briefly introduced as well as the notion of "scaled" drawings which allows a sketch to be measured for reference or estimating purposes. Finally, the various graphic conventions used in architectural floor plans will be covered.

Architectural Drawing Views

Three dimensional objects are depicted on paper by 2D drawings of three or more sides of that object. These "three or more" 2D *Views* allow someone to interpret the 3D image in their mind. This section will review the various views used in architectural drawing and design.

The simple object below describes the standard views used to describe the 2D drawings that are created for a 3D object. Looking at the 2D drawings below and then at the 3D object above you should be able to visualize how each represents the object under consideration. Of course things can get more difficult with complex objects, especially when it comes to architectural objects (i.e., buildings).

The exercises at the end of this chapter are provided as a way to help you to think three-dimensionally. For some it just comes naturally, and for others it takes a little practice. One thing you will find interesting with the exercises that follow is that totally different looking objects can have identical 2D views.

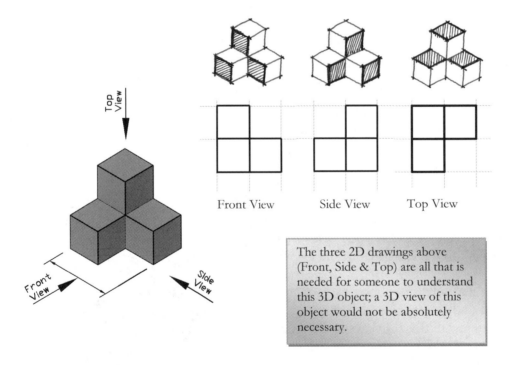

Front View   Side View   Top View

The three 2D drawings above (Front, Side & Top) are all that is needed for someone to understand this 3D object; a 3D view of this object would not be absolutely necessary.

Although you could imagine this object as an office building, the above example relates better to the world of *Mechanical Design and Drafting*. In the realm of *Architectural Drawing*, different terms are used to describe the views shown in the example above, and additional drawings, or *Views*, are often employed.

Exterior Elevations

The example below shows another simple object, but this time it clearly depicts an architectural example. In architecture, the vertical surfaces are illustrated in views referred to as elevations (exterior elevations to be specific); they are further defined by a direction modifier. For example, the exterior elevation which illustrates the walls facing south is referred to as the south elevation. Some "newbies" get a little confused because the view is actually looking north, but it looks at a wall(s) which is facing south!

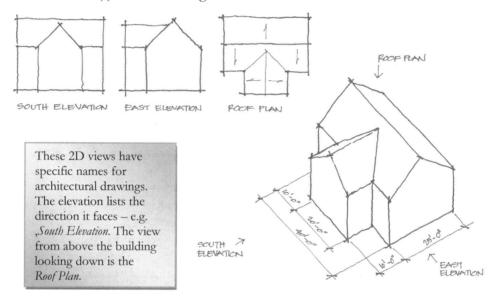

SOUTH ELEVATION   EAST ELEVATION   ROOF PLAN

These 2D views have specific names for architectural drawings. The elevation lists the direction it faces – e.g. *South Elevation*. The view from above the building looking down is the *Roof Plan*.

The images below further demonstrate the concept of how an elevation is a projection of a three-dimensional building. The sketch artist will utilize various line weights, shades and shadows to suggest depth in an otherwise flat 2D drawing. (This is true for both hand sketching and technical drawings.)

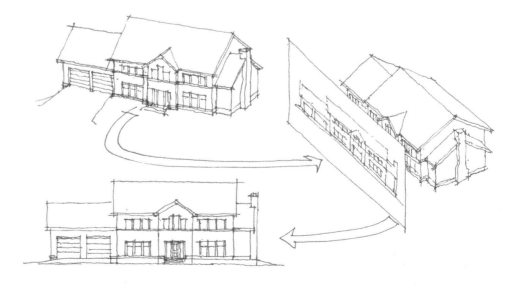

Floor Plans

In addition to the 2D views mentioned on the previous page which describe the outer-most faces of a building (i.e., Exterior Elevations), another set of 2D views reveal the elements within, called *Floor Plans* and *Sections*. Please read the information to the right in conjunction with the images shown below to learn more about these important views.

What is a Floor Plan – Image I
Imagine a plane which cuts through the building about 4 feet above the ground; this would be the cut plane

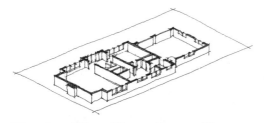

What is a Floor Plan – Image II
Imagine the portion of building above the "cut plane" being removed.

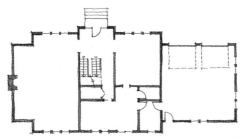

What is a Floor Plan – Image III
Result: Flattened 2D view from "cut plane" down.

2D Slices & Projections:
Architects use drawings to convey their ideas and design solutions to clients and contractors. This was true even when the Architect was the Master Builder and directly involved with the construction of a building. The drawings used today by contractors are legal, binding documents that the contractor must follow closely or risk legal or financial penalty. These drawings are primarily created using computers today, but for most of history, architectural drawings where created by hand drawing directly on paper.

The drawings created by an Architect or Engineer are typically 2D drawings, which makes sense as they are drawn on flat (i.e., 2D) pieces of paper. The 2D drawings, when considered as a whole, describe a building three-dimensionally. It takes instruction and practice to be able to create or even read these types of drawings, but the concept is quite simple. The 2D drawings are made up of what you might think of as slices or projections of the building in one of three axes: X, Y & Z.

One of the primary drawings used in architecture is the floor plan. As you can see in the illustration to the left, this drawing is a view from the top – totally flat – with the upper portion of the building cut-away (or ignored for clarity).

Floor Plans show the location of doors, windows, walls, stairs, cabinets, equipment, furniture and more!

Finally, imagine looking straight down on the cut-away building:
Another way to think about how a floor plan drawing relates to the actual
building is this: imagine taking a chainsaw and cutting horizontally, about four
feet above the floor, through the walls, all the way around your house (please
don't actually try this!). Then you remove the top portion with a crane. You then
climb to the top of the crane, which is positioned directly above the remaining
bottom portion of the house and you take a picture. That picture would look very
similar to a 2D floor plan of that house – only the picture would have some
perspective distortion where the floor plan would not.

Construction Documents:
The end result of a design project, in the drawing sense, is a set of formal
drawings (Construction Documents, or CD's) that become part of a binding legal
document a contractor will use to build your design. This formal drawing set is
created on the computer for speed and accuracy, but is entirely based on the
earlier sketches drawn by hand. The CD set may consist of 100's of sheets; the
total number depends on the complexity of the project and the level of detail
required.

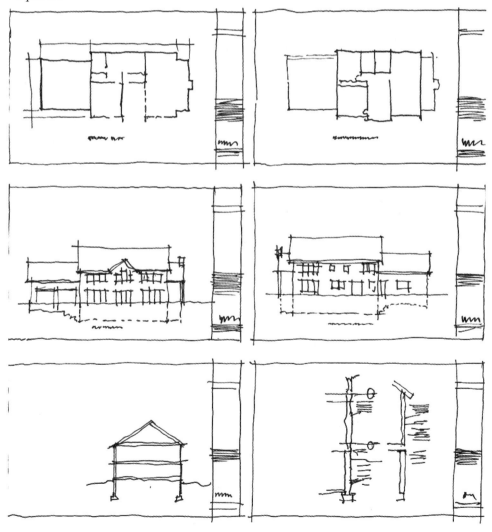

"True North" versus "Project North"

There are two more "big picture" aspects you should know about floor plans before moving on:

1. Drafted Floor Plans are always drawn to scale. This means that if you took the real version of the building and shrunk it, it would align with all the lines on the 2D floor plan drawing. The scale varies depending on the size of the building and the size of the paper; one example is ¼″ = 1′-0″ – this means that a line drawn ¼″ long on paper will equal 1′-0″ in the real world (a line 1″ long will represent 4′-0″ as there are four quarters in an inch).

   This is not as critical for hand sketches; however, an experienced designer can sketch [close to] proportionally accurate drawings. In other words, a 3′-0″ hallway is sketched about one-fourth the size of an adjacent 12′-0″ wide room. Proportionally accurate is more important than sketches being to scale.

2. With rare exception, modern drawings are oriented with project north upward on the paper; project north is not always the same as true north.

Project North Example:
The following real-world example illustrates the value of using the "project north" concept. In northern Minnesota, along the north shore of Lake Superior is a city which is generally stretched out parallel with the shoreline. As is turns out, all the streets run at an angle of almost 45 degrees off of "true north".

Rather than calling one end of the city the north-east end and the other the south-west end, a "project north" or plan north concept was embraced over time and one end is referred to as East and the other as West.

The "project north" concept, in this example, was implemented at a city wide level and has been subsequently used on all architectural projects.

Exception to the rule: the site plan is usually drawn with "true north" pointing straight up on the sheet, and the building rotated accordingly.

In conclusion to an overview of "project north" vs. "true north", the designer needs to be aware of N, E, S, W directions when looking at drawings and designing a building (especially, for example, if the roof is sloped and will be supporting solar panels so the maximum solar energy can be collected during the day). Plus, you will start seeing elevation drawings with directional labels in this book so this concept needs to be understood.

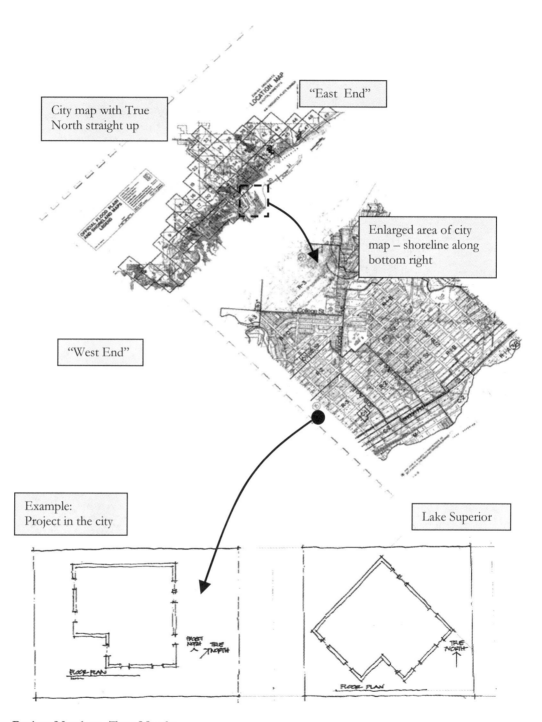

City map with True North straight up

"East End"

Enlarged area of city map – shoreline along bottom right

"West End"

Example:
Project in the city

Lake Superior

Project North vs. True North:
The image shown above is a standard architectural drawing sheet with the plan rotated to align with the sheet. Project North is straight up on the sheet and True North is about 45 degrees off. The sheet to the right shows the plan positioned on the sheet with True North pointing straight up on the sheet which would make the project difficult to draw and hard to read angled dimensions and such.

Sections

Like a floor plan, Sections are a cut-away view. The section reveals vertical relationships within the building.

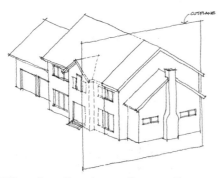

What is a Section – Image I
Imagine a plane which cuts through the building at a specific location.

What is a Section – Image II
Imagine the portion of building in front of the "cut plane" being removed.

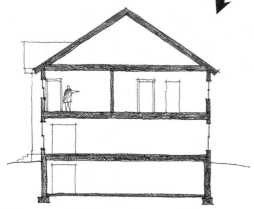

What is a Section – Image III
Result: Flattened 2D view from "cut plane" back.

Horizontal vs. Vertical Info:

Floor plans are the primary views used to convey relationships in the horizontal plane – for example: the distance between two walls, or the overall footprint of the building. It is not really possible to delineate relationships in the vertical plane – like the height from the floor to the bottom of a window (aka the window sill).

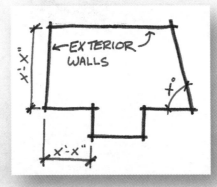

Elevations and Sections are the primary tools used to illustrate the various vertical relationships in a building – for example: the window sill, the distance between two floors or the roof's overhang.

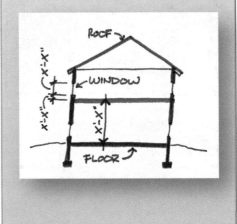

3D Views

Even though a good set of two-dimensional views can convey all required information to the contractor, both the client and contractor significantly benefit from one or more three-dimensional views. You will learn much more about 3D views later in this textbook, but right now they will be introduced to round off the discussion on views.

The image below is what you would refer to as a **Perspective View**. There are a few types of perspective views which you will learn more about later on. These types of views tend to be more life-like or photo-like than the isometric type 3D views covered below. Notice how the front of the building gets small as it moves back into the scene – even though the wall is the same height. Sketching this type of view will be a major focus of this book.

Example of a perspective View

Another type of 3D view is an **Axonometric View** as shown in the example below. This type of drawing looks distorted as compared to the perspective view above; however, it can be drawn to scale (at least partially) so dimensions could quickly be derived from it. An axonometric drawing can be quickly drawn with a plastic 30/60 triangle (i.e., the sides of the triangle are 30 degrees, 60 degrees and 90 degrees) and a T-Square or parallel bar on a drawing board.

Axonometric example by **Anne Porter CID**

Line weights

You will not need to use this information just yet, but we will plant the "seed" now regarding the concept and application of line weights. Lines of varying thickness will help convey the depth of the image (which is important in both hand and computer drawings); here are a few concepts to keep in mind:

- The perimeter of major building masses should have a heavy line to make it punch out from the surrounding image.
- When buildings have multiple "major elements" the line weights should vary. For example, two building dormers in the same plane should be the same line weight, but the lines should get lighter as they step back (i.e., away from the viewer).
- The next heaviest lines should be between materials (e.g., lap siding to brick) and around elements like windows and doors. These lines will also get lighter as they step back into the image.
- The lightest lines will be the ones which represent the various building materials (e.g., shingles, siding, brick, etc.).

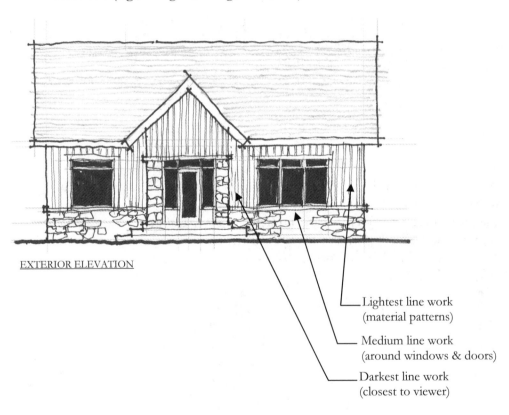

EXTERIOR ELEVATION

Lightest line work
(material patterns)

Medium line work
(around windows & doors)

Darkest line work
(closest to viewer)

Drawing Scale

Have you ever noticed the disclaimer on some cereal boxes which states that the picture has been enlarged to show texture of the product? They have intentionally made the product look larger than the actual size, or scale, of the product. Well, the opposite thing is done with architectural drawings. Architectural drawings are drawn at a fraction of the size of the real building, which makes sense as you would need a pretty big piece of paper to draw a building at actual scale. Rather than showing more detail (or texture), less is often shown for clarity. For example, the joints between the concrete blocks are not shown nor are the individual studs; instead just a representative space is shown with a hatch pattern to graphically represent each material type (concrete, studs, concrete block, etc.).

Not all hand drawings are drawn to scale. The early sketches are quick and loose and do not lend themselves to the time consuming task of laying down an architectural scale (not a ruler) and marking a specific length.

There are two main issues related to scaled drawings.

- **First** you need to assure your building will be buildable and meet the various building codes. If you did not draw to scale you could not be certain, for example, that all the furniture would fit in a particular room or that a sink/stove/dishwasher would fit into a length of countertop along a certain wall.

- **Second** you are constrained by the size of paper you intend to use. It is ideal to make the drawing as large as possible on the page, which allows for more detailed line work and notes and dimensions. However, only certain scales are typically used for certain types of drawings – like for plans, for example.

Here are the most used scales:

Architectural	Engineering
1/16" = 1'-0"	1" = 10'-0"
3/32" = 1'-0"	1" = 20'-0"
1/8" = 1'-0"	1" = 30'-0"
3/16" = 1'-0"	1" = 40'-0"
1/4" = 1'-0"	1" = 50'-0"
3/8" = 1'-0"	1" = 60'-0"
1/2" = 1'-0"	1" = 80'-0"
3/4" = 1'-0"	1" = 100'-0"
1" = 1'-0"	1" = 150'-0"
1 1/2" = 1'-0"	1" = 500'-0"
3" = 1'-0"	1" = 1000'-0"

Note: ' means FEET and " means INCHES

The image below will be used to cover how a scale is used and one method of determining what scale a drawing is (assuming you did not draw it).

Floor plans are typically drawn at ⅛″ = 1′-0″ or ¼″ = 1′-0″. So, assuming you did not draw this closet, you will try to determine what scale the drawing is. Is this closet drawn at ¼″ = 1′-0″ or is it drawn at ⅛″ = 1′-0″? Below the closet are two architectural scales (top two) and a ruler (the bottom one).

Question: how wide is the closet door if drawn at…

  ⅛″ = 1′-0″ _____   ¼″ = 1′-0″ _____

You will notice that each half tick on the ¼″ scale equals six inches; you can see that the closet door is two ticks or 1′-0″ wide (6″ x 2 ticks). Now looking at the ⅛″ scale we see that each tick is 1′-0″; thus, the closet door would be 2′-0″ wide if drawn at ⅛″ = 1′-0″.

Although possible, it is not likely that the closet door is only 1′-0″ wide. Even a 2′-0″ wide door is on the narrow side. So, we can conclude that the scale of this drawing is ⅛″ = 1′-0″. Knowing this you can see that the overall size of the space is 4′-0″. **FYI:** It is helpful to know that most doors on commercial projects are 3′-0″ wide, meeting the requirements for accessibility.

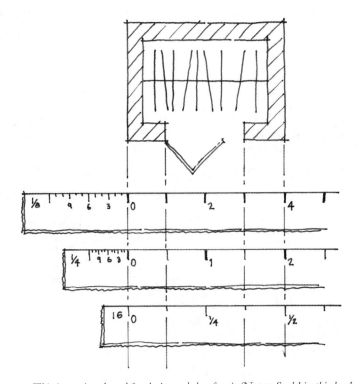

This image is enlarged for clarity and therefore is 'Not to Scale' in this book.

To make sure you get what is going on here, take a look at the image below. This is a sketch of a ¼″ scale (you do not always have to write or say the *equals a foot* part) and a ruler. This makes it clear what is meant by a ¼″ = 1′-0″; every quarter of an inch on the paper relates to 1′-0″ in the real world. Notice how 1′-0″ on the ¼″ scale aligns with ¼″ on the ruler above it? The 2′-0″ mark on the ¼″ scale aligns with the ½″ mark on the ruler – because (2) quarter inches equal 2′-0″ (or ½″ on the ruler). On a ¼″ scale drawing everything is scaled down to 1/48th of its actual size.

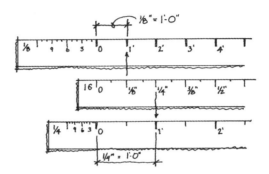

A contractor uses this information (i.e., drawing scale) to determine the quantities and cost of a building. So you can imagine how important it is to label drawings with the correct scale!

Which Scale to Use?

The next logical question is how is the correct scale selected? The list below indicates the most common scales used for each type of drawing. Ideally the largest scale possible would be used – the limitation being the size of the paper.

Common drawing scales used:

Floor Plan:	⅛″, ¼″
Enlarged Floor Plan:	¼″, ½″
Exterior Elevations:	⅛″, ¼″
Interior Elevations:	⅛″, ¼″, ½″
Building Sections:	⅛″, ¼″
Wall Sections:	½″, ¾″
Details:	½″, ¾″, 1″, 1½″, 3″

The details are the largest scale drawings because they represent a smaller part of the building (e.g., a roof edge vs. an entire floor plan) and show lots of details (e.g., flashing, rebar, fasteners, rubber roofing).

Although drawing to scale has a more limited role in hand sketching, it is still mandatory that the architectural designer understand this concept.

There are several types of scales (i.e., a tool for measuring distance) which can be purchased, so you need to understand the options before getting one.

Format/Units
First of all, there are architectural, engineering and metric scales. The engineering scales are used mainly by *Civil Engineers* and *Landscape Architects*. However, it is handy for the architectural designer to have one when drawing site plans. The metric scales are largely used by designers outside the United States, but are used on certain projects (e.g., US federal and military projects require them).

Shape/Size
Drawing scales come in all shapes and sizes. You can buy short ones (6″ to 12″ long) that are easy to carry around in a shirt pocket, briefcase or purse. In addition to being portable, the smaller scales are handy for measuring details and parts of larger drawings – for example, the clearances around a door in a floor plan.

These scales also come in sizes up to 36″ long (and longer) for drawing and measuring larger drawings. A scale this size can be used to measure the full length of a building plotted out on a sheet of paper (e.g., 24″x36″).

In addition to length, you should also consider the shape of the scale. Scales generally come in two shapes; triangular and flat. Each shape has its advantages and both are handy to have around.

The triangular shaped scale, shown to the left, is easy to pick up, lays flat on the drawing and has the most scales on it dues to the numbers of sides (6 total) given the shape.

Triangular Scale

Flat Scale

The flat scale, shown to the left, has the advantage of being portable as mentioned above. This scale can be a little more difficult to pick up off the drawing surface compared to the triangle which always has an edge pointing up with continuous grooves on each side making it easy to grasp. This scale only has four edges compared to the six on the triangle. It really comes down to preference more than anything, but many designers have and use both regularly.

Most architectural scales have two scales superimposed over each other – for example, ¼" and ⅛" share a common side of a triangular scale. Working from left to right is the ⅛" scale and from right to left is the ¼" scale. This means you have to pay attention to which numbers you are reading as one set is for the ⅛" scale and the other set is for the ¼" scale. The two sets of numbers are offset from each other to help keep things straight. The two scales on a face are always compatible in that one is twice the scale of the other; e.g., ½" and 1", ⅜" and ¾", 1½" and 3".

Looking at the image below, the arrows point at the numbers that relate to the 1" = 1'-0" scale. Notice how the other numbers are offset and are getting larger from the other direction (these would be for the ½" scale). The finer ticks to the right of 0 are the inches.

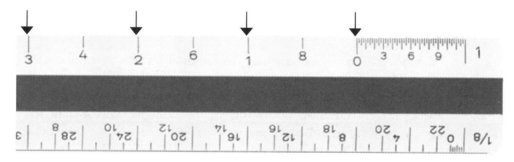

When you are measuring something, you align the closet whole foot number on one end and then see where the other end falls on the "inches" scale. In the example below the table is 2'-3" in length for a 1" = 1'-0" scale.

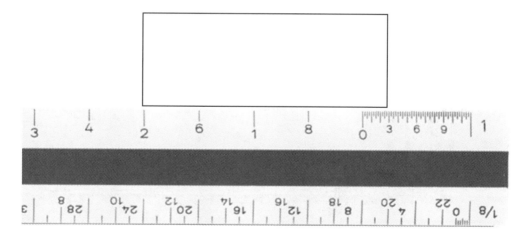

All architects and designers need to have a few drawing scales. Even the architectural technician who often mainly draws using the computer needs to be able to quickly measure the length of various lines on the printed page. At the very least, the scale is used to verify the plotter/CAD program printed the drawing the correct size.

Drawing Symbols/Graphics

When sketching Architectural drawings you need to be aware of a few basic graphic conventions for the major building elements like doors, windows, stairs, cabinets, and such. The drawings presented here can vary a bit from one designer/firm to another as far as line weight and embellishments, but for the most part everyone does it pretty much as shown here. Of course, we are talking about hand sketching here; when things get further along and are drawn in CAD/BIM, the symbols are more standardized and consistent.

When sketching preliminary floor plans, the walls, doors and windows are usually the only things drawn until you find a layout that looks like it will work. Then that option is refined with additional architectural elements like cabinets, plumbing fixtures (toilets, sinks, etc.), appliances and then even furniture.

Doors

Doors are an important part of any building design; their locations determine circulation, privacy, code compliance and more. In a floor plan, doors are usually shown open 90 degrees and an arc is added to indicate the swing. The swing arc is the path the door travels across the floor. Imagine attaching a piece of chalk to the outer edge of the door so it touched the ground and then you open the door; the line left on the ground by the chalk is the swing arc. The door is shown in the open position to indicate which direction it opens, which is important for circulation and code compliance, and to ensure the door does not conflict with other things such as cabinets, toilets, etc.

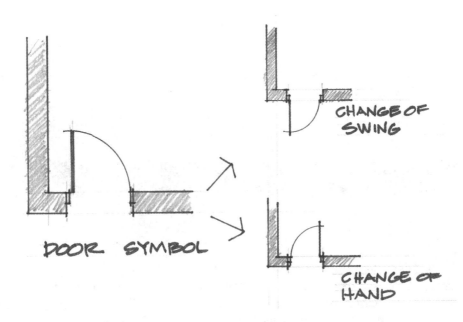

DOOR SYMBOL

CHANGE OF SWING

CHANGE OF HAND

Here are a few additional door graphics you might see or use in any given floor plan. Notice most show the door in an open position and have a swing arc line. Those that do not have a swing do not swing open. On commercial projects, as opposed to residential, the door frame is always shown.

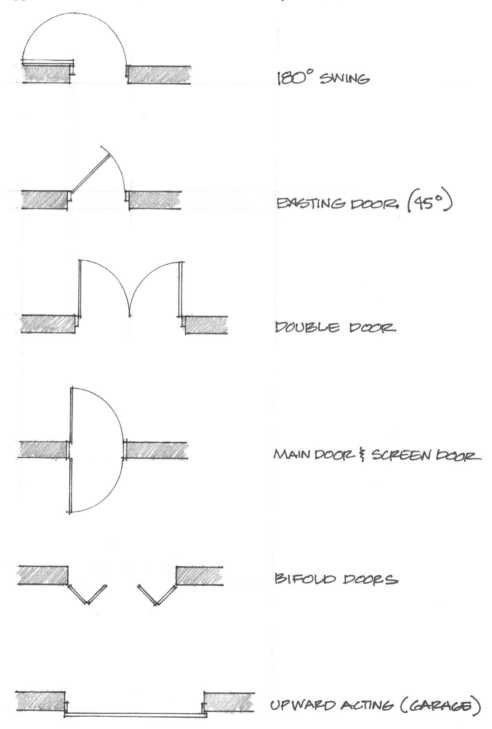

180° SWING

EXISTING DOOR (45°)

DOUBLE DOOR

MAIN DOOR & SCREEN DOOR

BIFOLD DOORS

UPWARD ACTING (GARAGE)

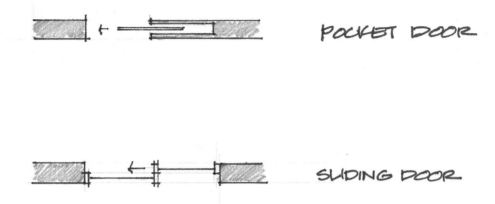

Windows

Another type of opening is the window. Early in the design process a very generic window is sketched – one line for each side of the window and a line parallel with the wall to represent the glass. As things become more developed, you can start adding mullions and frame depth and "location-in-wall" information.

FYI: All sysmbols drawn in this section have been hand drawn with a straight edge to make them crisp and less ambiguous. However, you will likely want to just sketch them by hand without the aid of a straight edge as that will slow you down. You can leave the straight lines for CAD/BIM.

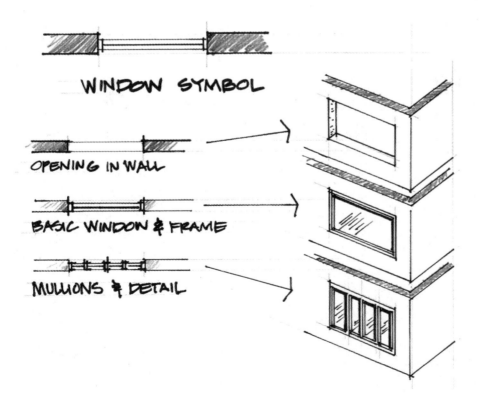

Plumbing Fixtures

As mentioned previously, plumbing fixtures are added once the plan becomes more finalized. It does not make sense to take the time to sketch in every little detail early on when you are still trying several different ideas. However, it is a good idea to show the plumbing fixtures (even in the sketching phase) so you don't forget how much room you need for the various toilets, sinks and such. Experience really helps here as the number of fixtures is based on various code requirements, and due to accessibility rules you may need twice the space you originally imagined. Figuring this out after the plan was thought to be "set in stone" and the structural, mechanical and electrical designers have begun their drawings is BAD! However, things are always changing right up until the last nail is hammered into the finished building, so it would not be totally unexpected.

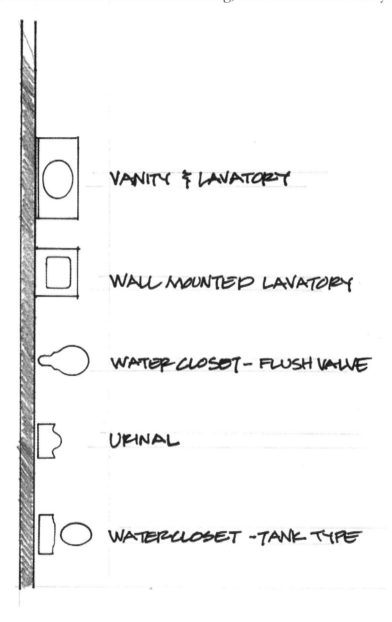

VANITY & LAVATORY

WALL MOUNTED LAVATORY

WATER CLOSET - FLUSH VALVE

URINAL

WATER CLOSET - TANK TYPE

Vertical Circulation: Stairs

Any building, residential or commercial, which has more than one floor or level has a stair with rare exception. Stairs take up a decent amount of floor space so you need to show them from the beginning of the design process and they need to be shown correctly. "Shown correctly" means the correct number of steps are shown (which meet building code) to get you from one floor to another – given the specific floor-to-floor height. You may not always know the exact distance between floors so you have to make an educated guess until you have more information.

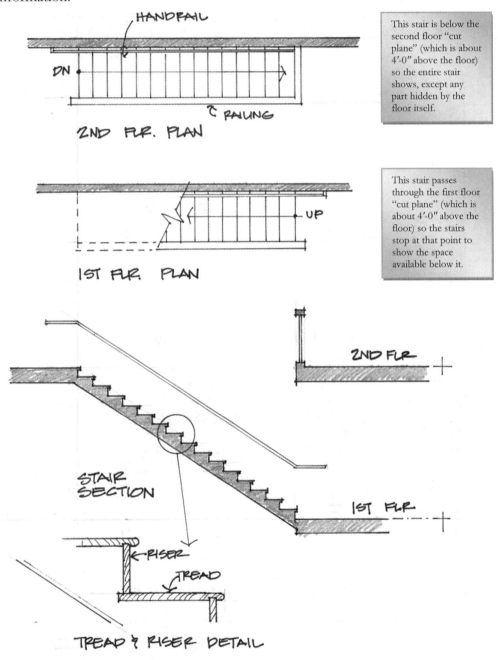

This stair is below the second floor "cut plane" (which is about 4'-0" above the floor) so the entire stair shows, except any part hidden by the floor itself.

This stair passes through the first floor "cut plane" (which is about 4'-0" above the floor) so the stairs stop at that point to show the space available below it.

Below are a few additional stair layouts. Many more scenarios could be shown but these cover the basics. Additional vertical circulation would include elevators, and space for their required machine room, and escalators.

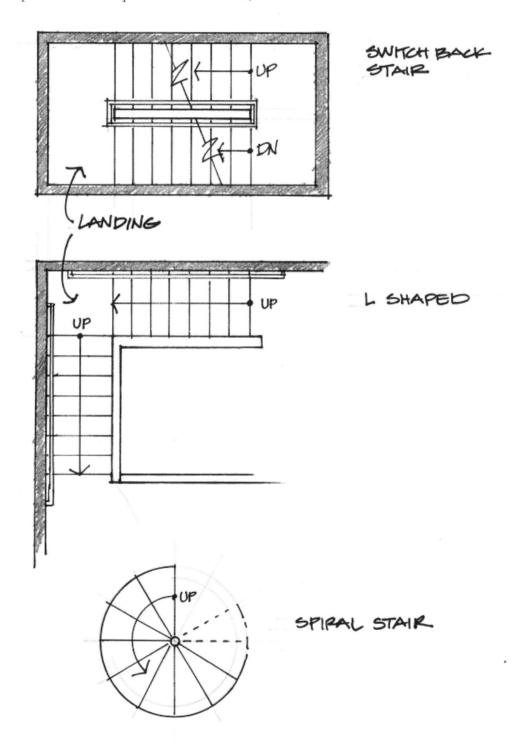

SWITCH BACK STAIR

LANDING

L SHAPED

SPIRAL STAIR

Casework: Cabinets

The goal in most architectural floors plans is to show anything that is fixed, built-in or otherwise not moveable; cabinets are one such thing. A few standard graphic conventions have been developed to show the various layered components of cabinets in a floor plan. Referring to the sketch below, and the one on the next page, you see the cabinets sitting on the floor, called **Base Cabinets**. They are drawn with solid or continuous lines. Base cabinets are typically 24″ deep. Next you have the cabinets above the base cabinets and attached to the wall, called **Wall Cabinets** (or Upper Cabinets). Wall cabinets are usually 12″-14″ deep and are drawn with a dashed line to indicate they are above. **Appliances** (i.e., refrigerator, range, dishwasher, etc.) are also shown and sometimes their doors are shown "dashed-in" while in the open position to make sure it does not conflict with something else.

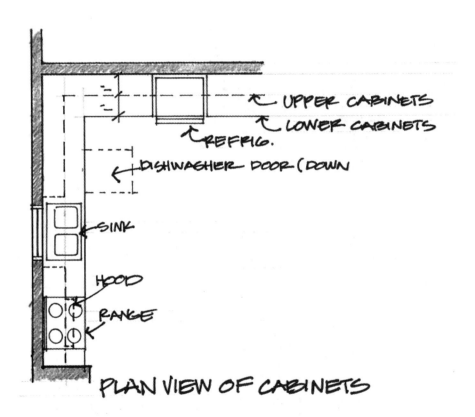

PLAN VIEW OF CABINETS

The information provided in this section just skims the surface on this topic. For an extensive study, you are encouraged to take a look at the **Architectural Graphic Standards** (Wiley, ISBN: 978-0-471-70091-3). Most every architect and architectural designer has this reference book which covers a large array of information, e.g., waterproofing, building details, masonry construction, gutter sizing, sports fields and much more!

This is not something that is usually hand drawn these days, but it is shown here to help you understand what exactly is being shown and discussed in the floor plan sketch on the previous page.

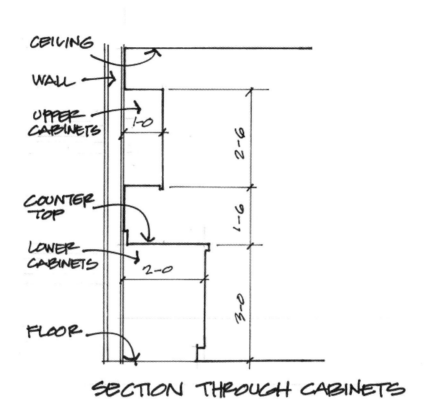

SECTION THROUGH CABINETS

Conclusion

This first chapter presented several fundamental concepts you need to know to get started in the world of creating architectural hand drawings. It is highly recommended that you complete the exercises that follow this chapter to make sure you "get it". If you have problems with the exercises, you should take a look at the videos on the DVD that come with this book and flip back through this chapter to see if you missed something. Also, the information here is meant to give you the knowledge and confidence to tackle the remaining chapters in this book. **NOTE**: It is recommended that you complete the chapters in order as they generally build upon each other. Finally, be sure you make time for reading and working on the exercises if you want to be really good at architectural drawing!

Don't forget about the videos

This book came with a DVD which contains several videos showing how to do several of the techniques presented. In the videos you see co-author Steve McNeill actually sketching, on bond and tracing paper, mostly using pen and colored pencil. The DVD should play in most comp0uters that have a DVD ROM drive. This DVD is not intended to be viewed on a home DVD player. The images below will give you a sample of what you can expect when you watch the videos…

Above: Photo of one of the video shoots for the videos bundled with this book.

Left: Screen shot of a video on the DVD.

Instructions: Chapter 2 exercises

These exercises are meant to help you look at a drawing on a piece of paper, which of course is a 2D drawing, and visualize its 3D shape. Sometimes you cannot fully comprehend a 2D drawing's complete 3D shape unless you have more than one view in which to reference. All views provided should have adequate information for you to complete the exercise.

The instructions provided below are for the exercises on the following pages – specifically, the Chapter 2 Exercises.

Match the small top, front and side views with the proper isometric view (i.e., the two large views). Write the *view type* (top, front or side) and the *isometric name* that view corresponds to (one example shown on the first exercise). Place a star on duplicate views for both isometric views; meaning the top view, for example, looks identical even though the 3D shape is clearly not identical.

The graphics below are repeated from the chapter as a reference.

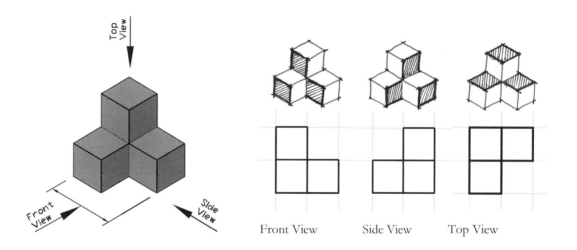

Front View   Side View   Top View

~blank page~

NAME_____ DATE_____

Exercise 2-1

1A

▼type:**Front** Iso:**1A**	▼type: Iso:	▼type: Iso:
	*	
*		
▲type: Iso:	▲type: Iso:	▲type: Iso:

1B

See page E2 for instructions.

Chapter **2** **EXERCISES**

~blank page~

NAME_____DATE_____

Exercise 2-2

2A

▼type: Iso:	▼type: Iso:	▼type: Iso:
▲type: Iso:	▲type: Iso:	▲type: Iso:

2B

See page E2 for instructions.

~blank page~

NAME_____DATE_____

Exercise 2-3

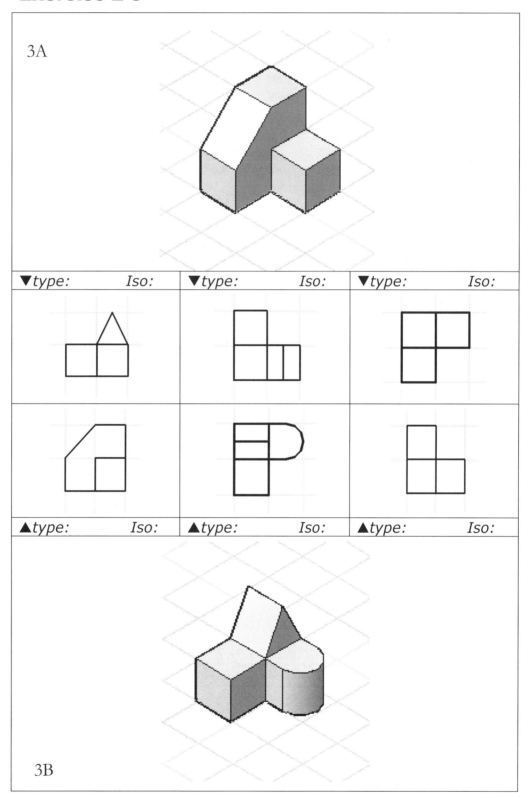

3A

▼*type:* Iso:	▼*type:* Iso:	▼*type:* Iso:
▲*type:* Iso:	▲*type:* Iso:	▲*type:* Iso:

3B

See page E2 for instructions.

~blank page~

NAME_____DATE_____

Exercise 2-4

4A

▼type: Iso:	▼type: Iso:	▼type: Iso:
▲type: Iso:	▲type: Iso:	▲type: Iso:

4B

See page E2 for instructions.

~blank page~

NAME_____DATE_____

Exercise 2-5

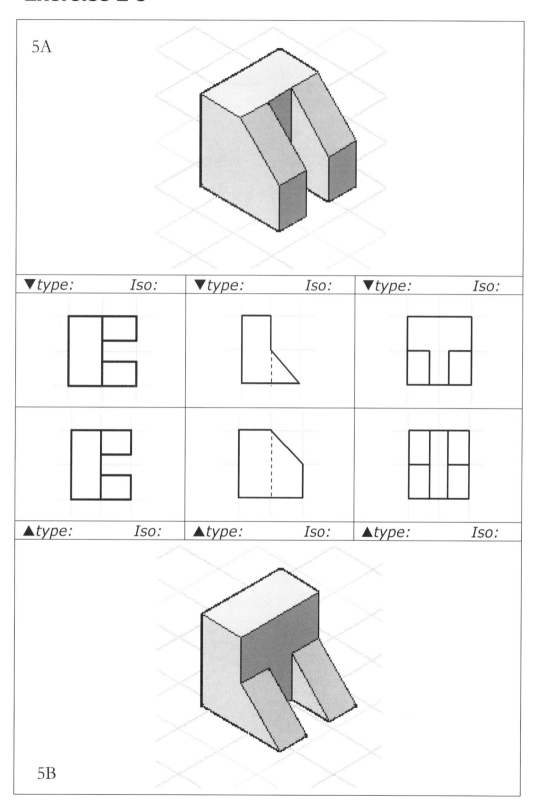

5A

▼type: Iso: ▼type: Iso: ▼type: Iso:

▲type: Iso: ▲type: Iso: ▲type: Iso:

5B

See page E2 for instructions.

~blank page~

NAME_____DATE_____

Exercise 2-6

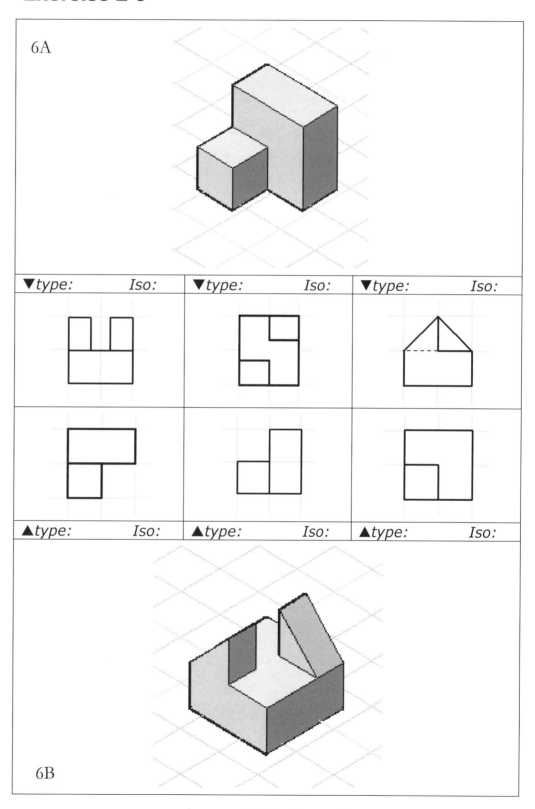

6A

▼type: Iso:	▼type: Iso:	▼type: Iso:

▲type: Iso:	▲type: Iso:	▲type: Iso:

6B

See page E2 for instructions.

~blank page~

NAME_____DATE_____

Exercise 2-7

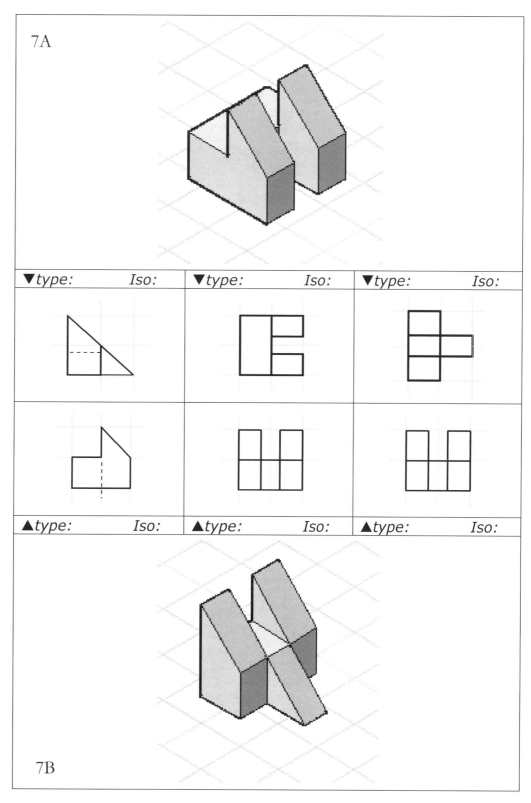

7A

▼type: Iso:	▼type: Iso:	▼type: Iso:
▲type: Iso:	▲type: Iso:	▲type: Iso:

7B

See page E2 for instructions.

~blank page~

NAME_____DATE_____

Exercise 2-8

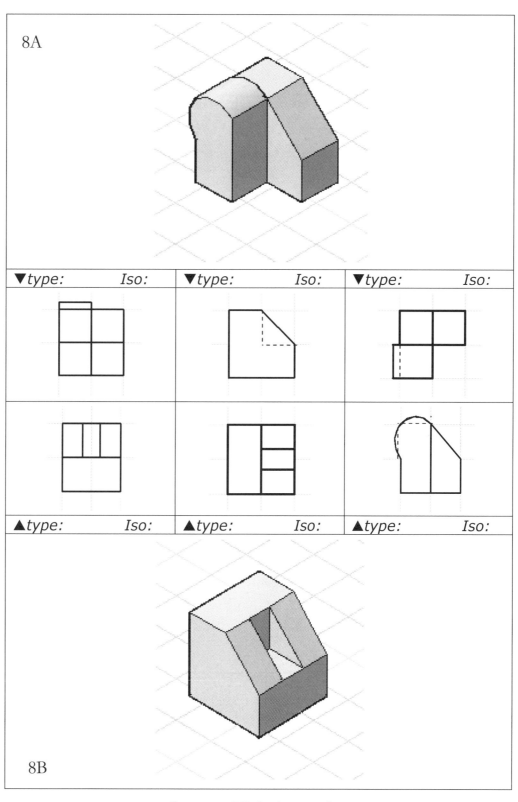

See page E2 for instructions.

~blank page~

NAME_____DATE_____

Exercise 2-9

This is a lightly drawn floor plan of a cabin or small home. Take a felt tipped pen, and using the conventions for windows, doors, cabinets & bathroom fixtures, sketch them in – using a straightedge or freehand – your choice. Be creative in your placement! Darken over the lightly drawn walls and infill or "poche" the walls with red or black pencil. Add hand written text to label the rooms.

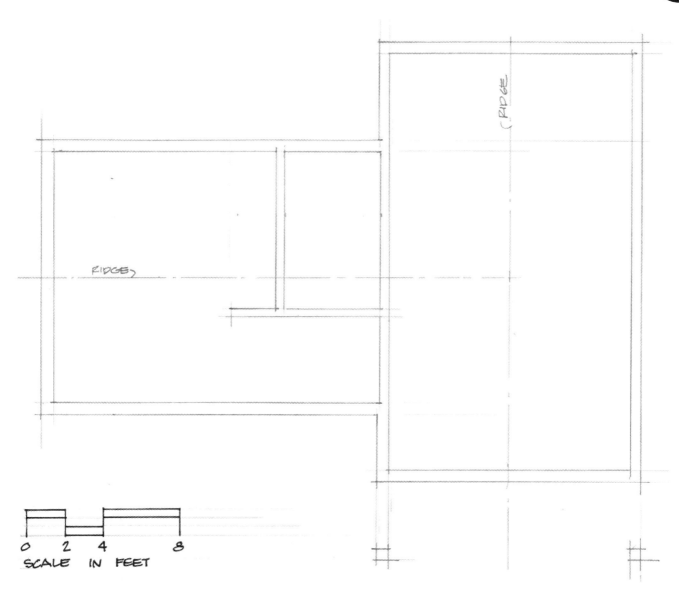

RIDGE

RIDGE

0   2   4   8
SCALE   IN   FEET

~blank page~

NAME_____DATE_____

Self-Exam:
The following questions can be used as a way to check your knowledge of this lesson. The answers can be found at the lower left on this page.

1. Every project has a True North. (T/F)

2. All sketches are drawn to scale. (T/F)

3. Less detail is typically shown for clarity. (T/F)

4. True North is always straight up on the paper. (T/F)

5. Line work closest to the viewer is heavier/thicker. (T/F)

Review Questions:
The following questions may be assigned by your instructor as a way to assess your knowledge of this section. Your instructor has the answers to the review questions.

1. 3D objects are depicted by three or more 2D views. (T/F)

2. Window sills are often dimensioned in floor plan views. (T/F)

3. The Architectural equivalent to Top View: _____ _____.

4. The type of drawing that looks most life-like: _____.

5. One of the primary views used in architecture: _____ _____.

6. Wall cabinets are drawn with a dashed line in floor plans. (T/F)

7. Name of drawing type that looks down on walls and floors.

    _____

8. Construction Drawings are use by contractor to build from. (T/F)

9. A 3D view drawn to scale: _____.

10. Did you remember to write your name at the top of the page? (Y/N)

*Chapter **2** Questions*

~blank page~

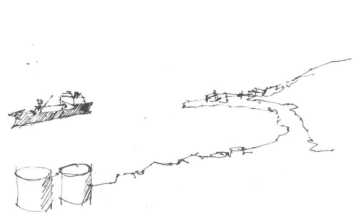

Getting Started

Where it all begins… the individual line. This chapter is dedicated to a formal discussion on this most basic component of a sketch. Though they surely studied it as a beginner, experienced designers rarely think about the fundamental concepts covered here; they have had enough experience and practice to have an intimate knowledge of these things.

The art of sketching is a learned talent. It is true some people seem to be a "natural" at it, but just like a stringed instrument, nobody really just picks it up and starts playing Tchaikovsky's Violin Concerto! So make sure you spend some quality time practicing – do all the exercises in this book plus come up with similar tasks you can try in a sketch book.

Think for a moment about the history of drawing. There were rather specific points in time when men developed techniques to make their drawings more life-like. Prior to these refinements, drawings were flat two-dimensional (2D) images (e.g., the Egyptian hieroglyphics).

Some of the topics covered in this chapter may seem pretty basic, but the discussion may reveal some subtleties you have not considered – so please bear with us!

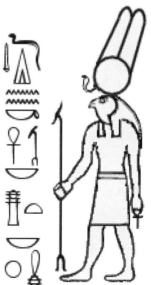

Image by **Jim Loy** © 2002
http://www.jimloy.com/
hiero/usrtsn.htm

The Line

The line is the beginning of all architectural drawing. It must define the edge of a wall, the corner or it is a part of a number of lines that defines a *hatch* or a *tone*. In short, it is the most basic "definer" that we use and hence the QUALITIES of this line can be very important.

The line must be done with an economy of time and effort. The sketch artist cannot waste too much time overanalyzing the technical aspects of each line one is drawing. Architectural projects often have tight budgets and short schedules – clients do not typically have bottomless pockets and would like to start utilizing their new facility as quickly as possible. Spending excess time sketching can eat into the design professional's profits and delay the project. So, the longer it takes to get your ideas on paper, the greater chance you have of that idea slipping away or you have less time to think about additional ideas.

Oh, and in the "real world" you are on the clock! Your boss is not going to pay you to just sketch all day and not get anything else done! The typical design professional still has to make time in the day to create the meeting minutes for the meeting with the client yesterday, meet with a product representative about a new roofing system they are promoting, and the list goes on and on. Thus, the problem is not so much wasting time sketching as it is not having enough time, so one is forced to use their time wisely.

What better way to analyze the fundamentals of the architectural lines than to use an architectural sketch of a six year old?

The sketch to the right clearly presents itself as a sketch of a building; it has walls, roof elements and a door. A hatch has even been added to better define the walls and perhaps a specific material.

A few key goals of this chapter are to plant the seed about ways to draw horizontal and vertical lines that are indeed horizontal and vertical, as well as equally spaced, when needed. Also, the line thicknesses change for various parts of the sketch.

Of course these are not things a six year old need concern himself with, but those reading this book most certainly should!

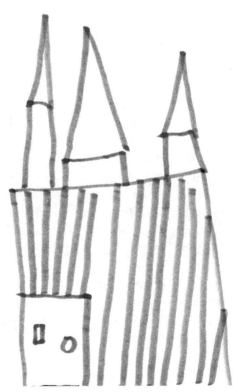

Six year old's sketch; Image by Carter Stine

The Horizontal Line

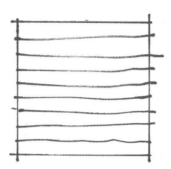

A handful of comments can be made about the horizontal line in the context of hand sketching – particularly freehand sketching. You are encouraged to read through this material and not just jump ahead to the exercises, especially if your instructor assigns the questions at the end of the chapter!

The most challenging thing about drawing a horizontal line is drawing a horizontal line; the line does not have to be perfectly straight but rather close to horizontal overall. Many are challenged with the eye-hand coordination required to keep a line horizontal on the paper when they are first learning to sketch. The main reason has to do with how your body is designed and the result is that you have to adjust your wrist and/or elbow as you move your pencil across the paper (this is not really a problem for vertical lines – discussed a little later).

Therefore, the natural "arc" of the hand can limit stroke lengths. At a certain point you find the need to make an adjustment in your hand position to keep your horizontal line on track. This results in a "kink" in your line. Rather than a "kink" that tends to look like a mistake you can overemphasize the transition by lifting the pen/pencil and leaving a small gap – even adding a little extra pressure at the beginning and end of each stroke…

Another method that can be employed when developing horizontal lines is an intentional (even exaggerated) squiggle in the line. This can effectively hide the "adjustments" that are needed to keep the line on track (i.e., horizontal).

Horizontal lines on a surface in perspective have some additional challenges which will be covered later in this textbook.

A squiggly line intentionally added at the roof edge.

The Vertical Line

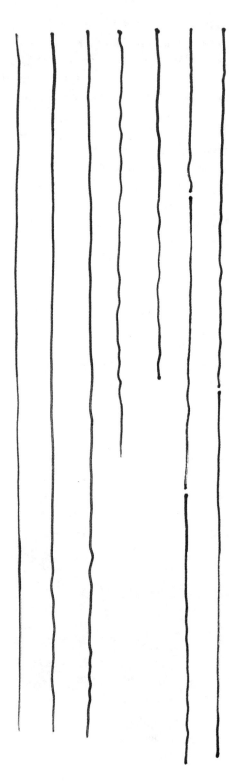

Unlike the horizontal line, the vertical line is not so much limited by the "arc" of the hand and therefore is easier to do. You still need to practice a little eye-hand coordination to keep the line vertical. These lines are often drawn downward, unlike "drafted" vertical lines which are usually drawn from the bottom up.

> **Drafted** means a drawing was created with tools such as straightedges, triangles, and parallel bar in order to create accurate, crisp lines. In contrast, a **Sketched** drawing does not employ much more than the pen as illustrated in the image below.

Even though vertical lines are easier to draw than horizontal lines, you may still want to add gaps between smaller strokes, which will add a little "snap".

Your vertical lines can be straight or have some intentional squiggle which allows for more fluid movement.

Lines to Avoid

In order to get a better feeling for the qualities of a "good" line we will point out some less desirable lines and techniques. No one is suggesting that there is a "right way" and a "wrong way" to create architectural drawings – but, honestly, there are "good" drawings and "not so good" looking drawings; some that are generally clear and easy to understand and some that are ambiguous and amateurish. So the goal here is to point you down the path that most seasoned architectural designers travel and find success.

One line to avoid is the "scrubbing" line. This would be great as the outline of a lion, but architecturally you would rarely use a line like the one below. This resultant "scrub" type line is often the natural inclination one has to assemble a series of line stokes.

Another line to avoid is one that starts out weak, then heavy and then weak again. A line should usually be constant in thickness and can even have its start and end points emphasized so it appears very intentional.

When lines come together to form the corner of a wall in a floor plan or the peak of a roof in elevation, architects and designers usually extend the lines so they cross – which develops an unmistakable corner. Most sketches are not meant to be works of art, rather they are a tool in which to communicate a design solution to other people (usually the client or the public), so drawing "outside the lines" is actually encouraged! If you take a look at the image below, you will find this line lacks consistency and crossing corners (a good example will be shown next). Finally, notice how the shape below is simply four individual lines – looked at individually you can see the "weak" line just mentioned above.

Good Lines

To balance things out we will now take a look at a few positive attributes you should be shooting for when sketching a line. Keep in mind we are talking about freehand sketching at the moment, not lines generated with the aid of a straight edge (i.e., drafted). You are shooting for "good" lines, not "perfect" lines…

You are encouraged to have a sketch book open and lying beside you as you read so you can try a few techniques. This will give you a little practice before you get to the exercises which need to be turned in (if using this book in a classroom setting). In your sketch book, try these concepts with both a pencil and a pen; many designers typically use a pen for most exploratory sketches as the lines are always crisp and you don't have to stop and sharpen the pencil.

Directly below is a sketched rectangle which has clearly defined corners and nice consistent lines. Notice that the lines usually start and end with a little heavier dot that is created by applying extra pressure. This line was created with a pencil, using ink is even easier to emphasize the ends.

As previously discussed in the section on horizontal lines, the wrist has a natural tendency to pivot. Therefore, this natural pivoting of your hand tends to want to arch, thus the ease with which the arc can be drawn (but not without some concern for accuracy if you need it).

Angled Lines and Hatching

The next logical topic for discussion is straight lines which are neither horizontal nor vertical: that is, angled lines. These lines are often used for contrast in a sketch – to shade one side of an object so the various faces stand out from each other – or to represent shadows. Taking this concept a bit further, we find this technique being used in more technical drawings to represent various materials – we refer to this as hatching.

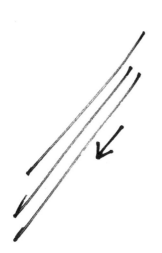

The **Diagonal Line** is typically drawn in a downward stroke.

The diagonal line is a basic building block of shading and hatching patterns. You can create many different looks by varying the spacing or angle and pencil or pen weights.

One way to very quickly control a series of diagonal lines and turn into a hatch is to place a triangle, straight edge or similar clear ruler and draw a series of closely spaced diagonal lines against it… creating an open, yet crisp edge.

Connecting strokes on a diagonal line is fairly difficult and not that pleasing visually. It is often easier to use very short strokes and slightly change directions as shown here. As you look at the older illustrations using pens, you will often see this sort of technique and will come to appreciate the tonal qualities it can impart.

The **Cross Hatch** is quite simply the overlay of two diagonal directions. Often the second (or cross) hatch can be only partial or over a certain area, giving depth and variety to the effect.

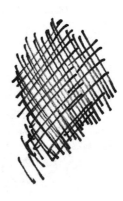

Below are a few other variations on hatching. The upper left box shows more of a "technical" hatch in that it is used on details and working drawings (often referred to as Blue Prints – even though they are not blue anymore). The lower left and middle right are the result of rubbing the lead over the paper while it has a heavily textured material beneath it; this results in a consistent and interesting pattern.

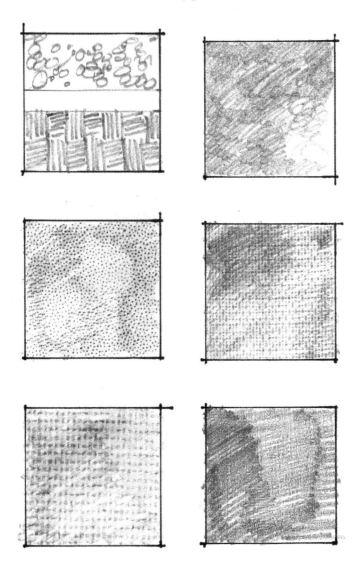

Gesture Drawing

One of the biggest hurdles many have to becoming decent delineators is moving the instrument (pencil, pen, etc.) quickly and loosely on the paper. Too often the would-be designer is sketching slowly and overanalyzing even the earliest strokes. Therefore the next discussion, and subsequent exercises at the end of the chapter, are designed to address this challenge.

Gesture drawing is the process of sketching quick, playful lines on paper while leaving the pen in contact with the paper most of the time. The goal is to create a close approximation of an object (real or imagined) with an economy of time.

With practice your gesture drawings will start to have the proper proportions and poses that will enhance the "scene" of your perspective drawings later on in this book. Again, right now this is just a pragmatic exploration in putting pen to paper!

Architecture is really about the interplay of people and buildings; drawing a building with no people is like drawing a car with no tires. Quickly sketched human forms give your drawings scale and life. They can be used, as will be discussed later, as a method of perspective drawing called *"the human measuring stick method"*.

The exact way in which a *gestured person* is drawn is really up to the individual, but a few tips will be provided here to help get you started. With a little practice and effort you can develop your own style, which can be one of the "trademarks" of your drawings.

Sketching a basic figure, perhaps like the one shown below, can start with a head oval (which is often aligned with the horizon line – more on this later), then the quick body trunk which morphs into the legs with no feet. Next you add arms that omit the hands. The position of the arms and legs often imply a certain activity (walking, sitting, pointing) or situation (assembly, excitement, peace). Finally one might choose to add hatch or tone with diagonal lines (just covered) or swirly lines which give the figure dimension; and maybe some are hatched and others left as outlines which creates contrast and can imply racial diversity amongst the buildings occupants.

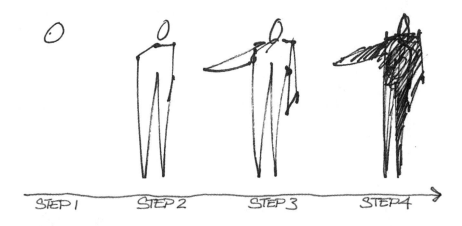

Similar steps can be used to create a gesture drawing of a seated person. Focus should be placed on the larger body elements such as the torso, thighs, calves, etc. Next you can add "props" like a chair or a briefcase (see example on previous page) to give the figure additional dimension or meaning.

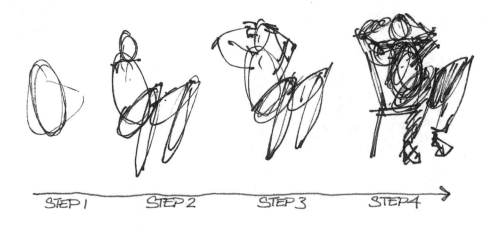

Remember to stay fluid and work very quickly. In fact this exercise should focus on speed to capture the essential "massing" of the human form. If you are working through this book in a classroom setting, you may be asked by the instructor to do some in-class exercises where everyone has, let's say, one minute to sketch a person being displayed on the overhead projector. Several images can be displayed and each drawn within the time constraint. Of course you can do this on your own using a magazine and your sketch book. Either way this would be great practice before trying the gesture exercises at the end of this chapter.

Just as people can be quickly "gestured" in a drawing, so too can building masses, forms and ideas be rapidly done. Below is an example of a small building; note the multiple quick lines and no scrubbing. Practicing in a sketchbook on small, simple buildings, in conjunction with great speed will help develop an ease with the medium (i.e., paper) and tools (e.g., pen or pencil).

Quick simple bold lines portray the building, the tree and the land form.

Gesture sketching just for fun…

Image directly above by Architect Alan Anderson

The images on this page provide examples from two architects' sketch books.

The image above, by co-author McNeill, is a loose lunch-time sketch of a visiting ship in the Duluth harbor.

The image to the left is a page with multiple studies nestled together on one page; these quick sketches are meant for practice and therefore do not need to be neatly arranged on separate pieces of paper.

Even architects with years of experience find time to practice…

Using the gesture technique in sketching up a floor plan is an all important tool to place an idea on paper. Note the door drawn over the wall lines. This is not a problem (and no need to erase anything); just darken the walls to the side of it to emphasize the opening. This, again, is a very quick exercise intended for study and analysis – not a drawing you would likely show a client (unless you where meeting with the client and sketching in front of the client).

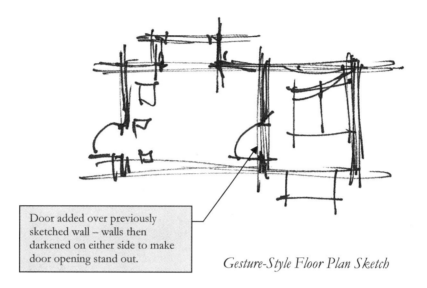

Door added over previously sketched wall – walls then darkened on either side to make door opening stand out.

Gesture-Style Floor Plan Sketch

In addition to getting ideas onto paper there are a few additional reasons for employing this "gesture" type sketching method for buildings and floor plans. One is when walking through a building for the first time (maybe you will be designing an addition or remodeling); by sketching the location of walls and doors you are enhancing your memory of each space by putting pencil to paper. Taking digital pictures certainly helps, but architects, designers and technicians usually have the ability to think three-dimensionally, so sketching reinforces one's grasp of a space. Once back at the office, the sketches can be reviewed for the purposes of writing a memo about the meeting or to develop an estimate for your services.

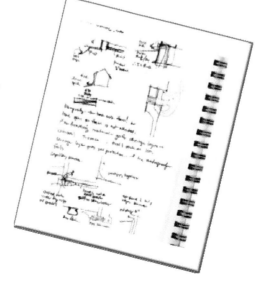

Also, quick sketching is helpful when attending seminars. This sketch book page (to the right) is from a Radon Gas presentation. The sketches may never be directly looked at again, but simply having sketched it helps one engrave that concept or image in their mind for future retrieval.

Hand Lettering

The art of hand lettering is not as admired as it once was. Most of what you read these days is presented in typed format, generated using a computer and printer. There is certainly nothing wrong with computer generated lettering, and some of us really benefit from the spell-check functionality! However, the would-be architectural designer would do well to practice hand lettering and develop a lettering style. The designer will often find one's self sketching in front of the client or contractor and should be able to create clean legible text that looks professional.

Most designers are rather particular about their lettering style; this also applies to their signature. It is interesting that many designers have two lettering styles – one for presentation drawings and the other for personal and inter-office notes. The latter is barely legible, even by the author! The "sloppier" lettering style has to do with the fact that the brain works faster than the hand and pen – so designers, much like doctors, tend to have lots of horizontal lines that appear to jump up and down and roughly form words (this is a bit of an exaggeration, but you get the point)!

A presentation-type lettering style is usually preceded by two light horizontal lines which are used as guidelines; the typical text height is 3/16″ for notes (when generated by a computer, like a CAD system, the text height is often 3/32″; due to the consistency and accuracy of the computer and printers it is still easy to read and takes up less room. This may seem elementary, but it helps to create nice, crisp, horizontal lines of text where the tops and bottoms are well proportioned and aligned.

The instrument used to generate the letters is just as important as the style. As you can see below, the top example in which a **pen** was used produced a bolder and crisper look as compared to the second example created with **pencil**. The third example used a heavy **felt tip pen**. So you may have created a sketch in pencil but maybe the text should be in pen to make to "punch out" more; or if you sketched in pen, maybe the text is done with a heavy felt-tipped pen.

Most architectural hand lettering is uppercase. Beginning on the next page you will see the lettering style of a few different architects. Notice the various little embellishments that make each unique. In the exercises at the end of this chapter you will have the opportunity to practice hand lettering. Throughout this book you should try to place an emphasis on hand lettering, labeling drawings and even just adding your name and the date to the pages to be turned in.

In the past, primarily before computers were common place, all text was hand written. Text, such as titles, firm names and such, was often generated with a pen or pencil and an aid, such as a stencil or transfer sheet. With modern technology most all of the formal title can be generated by the computer, which makes for a clean, crisp and professional presentation. Hand lettering for formal presentations should be limited to notes and minor labels. Much like the way this textbook was prepared, one can scan hand sketches and place them in a document with computer graphics and text.

Hand sketched image with computer generated text; also take note of the "gesture" people.

Image Used by Permission

Below (and on the next page) are several examples of hand lettering styles:

Example #1: *Dan Stine (as a student in1992)*

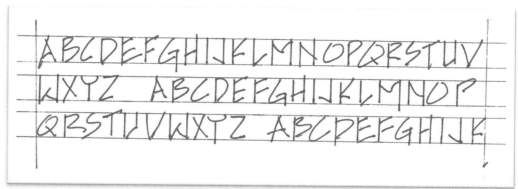

Example #2: *Larry Turbes*

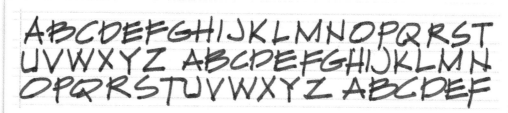

Example #3: *Alan Anderson*

Example #4: *Craig Schneuer*

Example #5: *Mark G. Poirier*

Another example, in the sketch below, is hand lettering used to note materials and list lengths. Notice that zero inches are always listed and everything is capitalized.

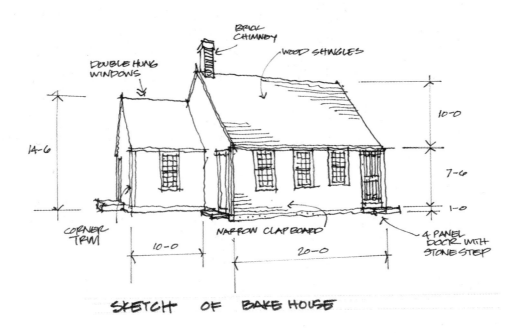

Lines and Hatching applied

Below are two birch bark study sketches which use several of the techniques discussed in this book, including lines and hatching.

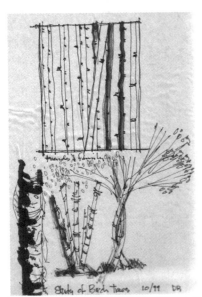

Birch Study Sketches by **Darryl Booker**,
Associate Professor, North Dakota State University

NAME_____ DATE_____

Exercise 3-1

It is recommended that you tear these pages out at the perforated edge, one at a time, before you use them so you can lay them firmly on a smooth surface as you work. You can then add your name and date above and turn in to your instructor.

It is important to learn to handle your pencil and/or pen properly to create the desired line or shape. The following tasks will walk you through several fundamental steps in sketching. Only use a pencil (or pen) for these "Chapter 3" exercises (no straight edges).

Equally Spaced Horizontal Lines using a pen

In this first task you will draw equally spaced horizontal lines. One goal is to learn how to move your hand as you draw so the line stays horizontal; the other is to visualize where to place your pencil on the paper so the next line will be equal distance as compared to the previous lines. *The lines do not have to be perfect, so do this quickly!*

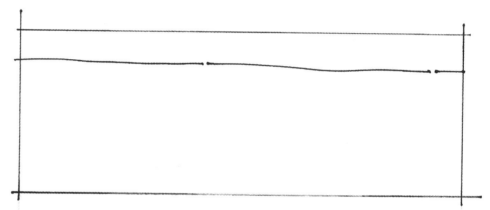

Next draw equally spaced horizontal lines, making them twice as close (in spacing) as the previous example. *Do this quickly!*

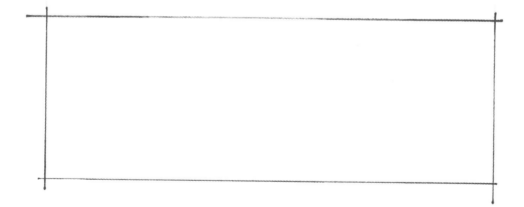

~blank page~

NAME_____ DATE_____

Exercise 3-2

Equally Spaced Vertical Lines using a pen

Follow the space steps in the previous exercise, but sketch vertical lines. Do not simply turn the page 90 degrees and sketch horizontal lines; this is often not possible as the paper is too large or it is taped to the drawing board. Do this three times in the boxes provided. You may want to try it a few times in a sketch book or on the back of some old printer paper first.

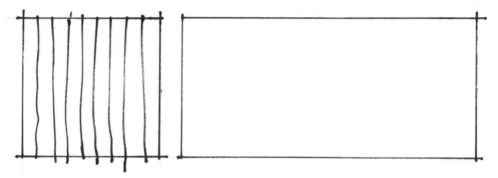

This is the example

Draw equally spaced vertical lines using a consistent line weight.

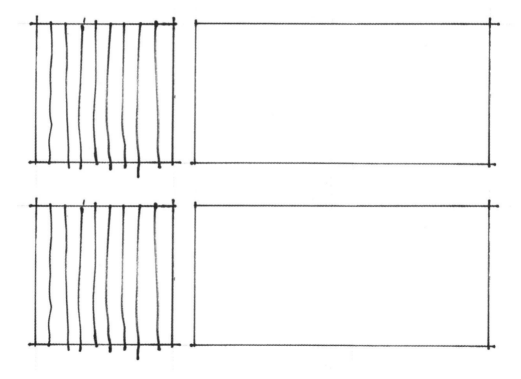

~blank page~

NAME_____ DATE_____

Exercise 3-3

Equally Spaced Vertical Lines using a pencil

Here you will sketch additional vertical lines - the only difference is that you will use a pencil rather than a pen. Take the time to note the difference in line quality and tone.

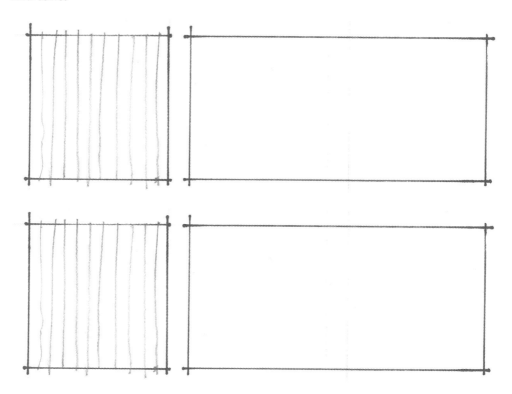

In this last box, apply varying degrees of pressure to vary line weights.

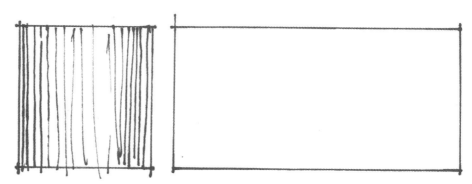

~blank page~

NAME_____ DATE_____

Exercise 3-4

Tightly Spaced Vertical Lines using a pen
Here you will sketch additional vertical lines – the objective is to use the finest tipped pen you have and sketch closely spaced lines. This should still be done quickly while moving lightly! A series of lines like this can be used to represent the texture of a buildings material (e.g., brick, lap siding, corrugated roofing) or shades and shadows in a more abstract way.

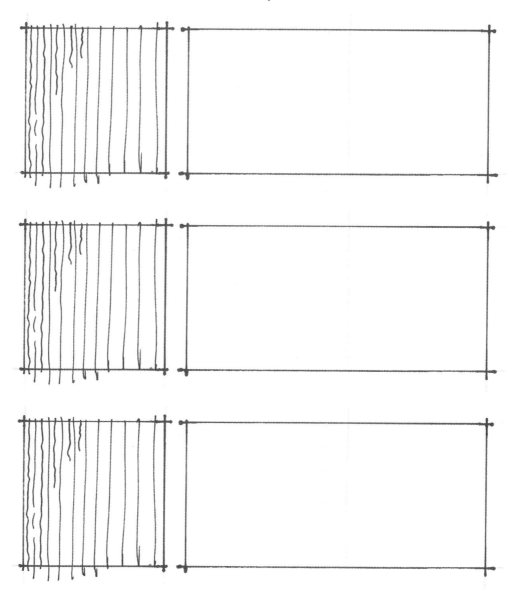

~blank page~

NAME_____ DATE_____

Exercise 3-5

Long Vertical Lines using a pen

Continue to practice sketching vertical lines that are evenly spaced – pick your spacing. Don't be afraid to add a little squiggle to your lines as discussed previously in this chapter. Remember: move quickly and only free-hand.

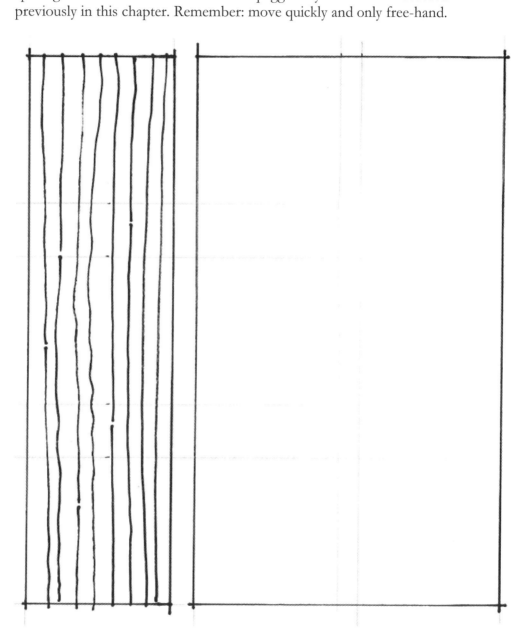

Chapter **3** EXERCISES

~blank page~

NAME_____ DATE_____

Exercise 3-6

Equally Spaced Diagonal Hatch

In this task you will draw equally spaced diagonal lines. Follow this pattern to complete the other two tasks below (on this page).

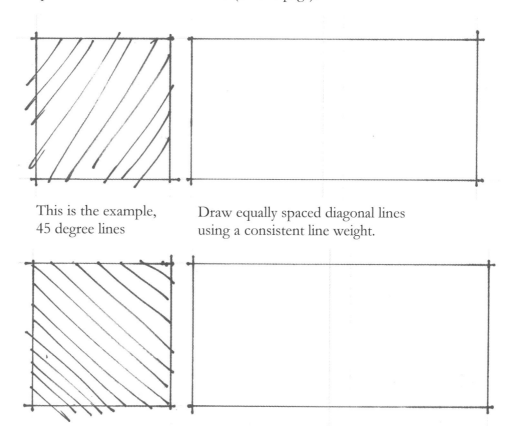

This is the example, 45 degree lines

Draw equally spaced diagonal lines using a consistent line weight.

Irregular Diagonal Hatch

Using quick hand movements, sketch an irregular hatch pattern as shown below in the example square (on the left).

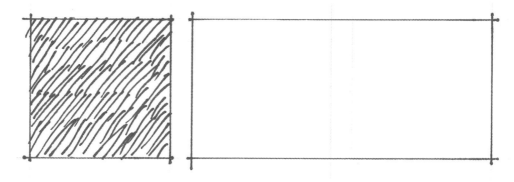

~blank page~

NAME_____ DATE_____

Exercise 3-7

Additional Hatch Patterns
Draw the hatching as shown in the space provided.

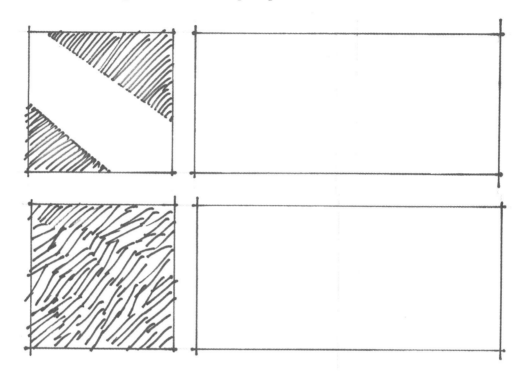

Cross Hatch
Add a set of diagonal lines (45 degrees) in each direction. This pattern is used in sketches to represent shadows and glass; in details it is rigid insulation.

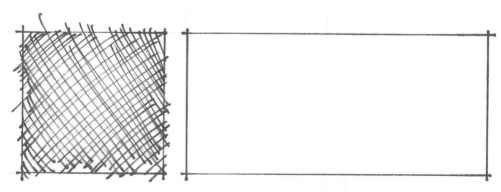

~blank page~

NAME   DATE

Exercise 3-8

Additional Hatch Patterns

Sketch the hatch patterns shown in the space provided to the right. The top example, as you will recall from this chapter, shows gravel over an earth hatch pattern. The bottom example is the result of "rubbing" the pencil over the paper with a heavily textured material below the paper – which means you should first remove the paper from the book and place over a heavily textured material to complete this exercise!

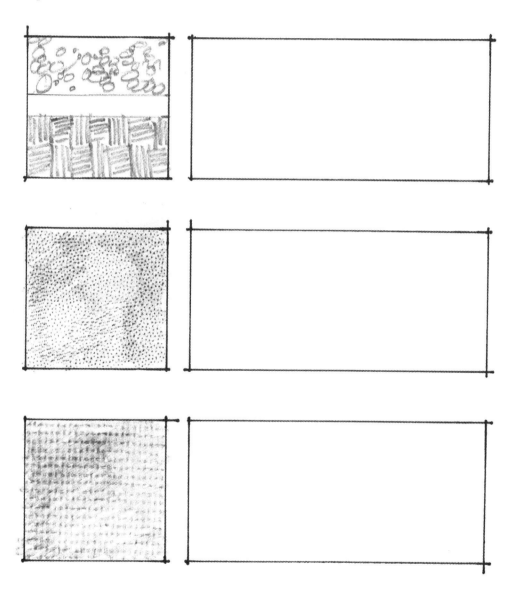

~blank page~

NAME_____ DATE_____

Exercise 3-9

Additional Hatch Patterns
Sketch the hatch pattern shown in the space provided to the right. Use the techniques covered in this chapter.

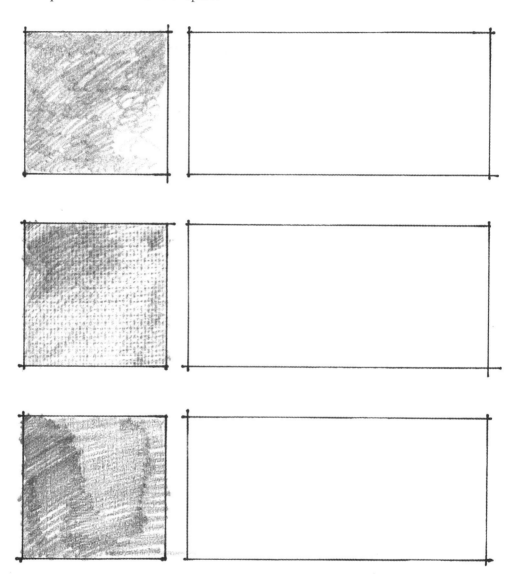

~blank page~

NAME_____ DATE_____

Exercise 3-10

Equally Spaced Long Horizontal Lines

In this task you will draw longer horizontal lines – the goal is to pay attention to not resting your palm on the paper; rather keep it moving with the pencil and anticipate any adjustments needed to keep the line horizontal. Try to keep things fast and loose – do not erase anything.

More Horizontal Lines

Continue drawing long horizontal lines in the boxes below. Try this technique for creating equally spaced lines: sketch the first line in the middle and then draw the next line centered between that line and the edge. Continue this process in each direction until you cannot add any more lines.

Aligned Horizontal Lines

Follow the steps in the previous box, but make the lines line up between boxes. Try drawing one continuous line, lifting your pencil to skip to the next box.

~blank page~

NAME_____ DATE_____

Exercise 3-11

Equally Spaced Long Vertical Lines
Same as the previous tasks, just vertical
lines. Line work like this is often used to
represent materials on the surface of
your building, for example: brick, siding,
roofing, etc.

~blank page~

NAME_____ DATE_____

Exercise 3-12

Quickly Sketch Circles

Use the square to aid in drawing an accurate circle – focus on a quarter of the circle at a time. Each quadrant of the circle fits the midpoints of the edges of the squares. **FYI**: You will apply this technique again later in the book, but onto a surface in perspective.

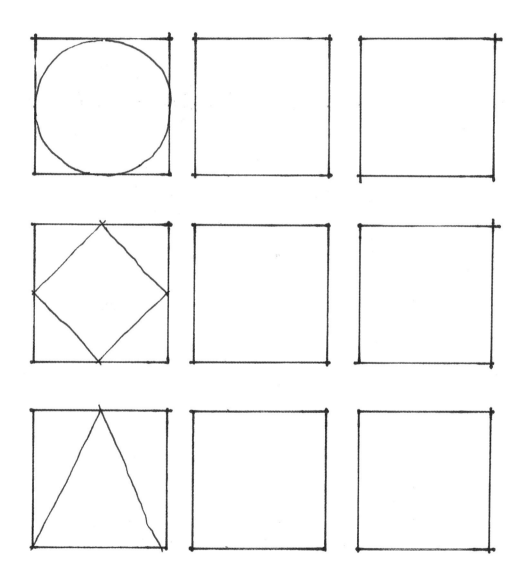

~blank page~

NAME_____ DATE_____

Exercise 3-13

Practice Gesture Drawing: People
As discussed in this chapter, you need to practice quick and loose sketching of people and small simple buildings. These gesture drawings should each be done in less than two minutes.

Quickly sketch the figures above in the boxes below.

~blank page~

NAME_____ DATE_____

Exercise 3-14

Practice Gesture Drawing: People
As discussed in this chapter, you need to practice quick and loose sketching of people and small simple buildings. These gesture drawings should each be done in less than two minutes.

Quickly sketch the figures above in the boxes below. ..

~blank page~

NAME_____ DATE_____

Exercise 3-15

Practice Gesture Drawing: People
As mentioned in the previous exercise, these gesture drawings should each be done in under two minutes.

~blank page~

NAME_____ DATE_____

Exercise 3-16

Practice Gesture Drawing: Buildings
Try sketching this small building in a gesture type format; try using a felt tip pen and give yourself about 3-5 minutes tops. Don't worry about the little details.

~blank page~

NAME_____ DATE_____

Exercise 3-17

Practice Gesture Drawing: Buildings

Try sketching this small building in a gesture type format; try using a felt tip pen and give yourself about 3-5 minutes tops. Don't worry about the little details.

~blank page~

NAME_____DATE_____

Exercise 3-18

Practice Gesture Drawing: Floor Plans

Quickly sketch a "gesture" floor plan of the space you are in. Note doors and windows but move quickly – get it down! Again, this is an exercise in time efficiency. Give yourself 3-5 minutes of time to complete the drawing.

EXERCISES

Chapter 3

~blank page~

NAME_____ DATE_____

Exercise 3-19

Practice Architectural Lettering

Use the space provided below to practice hand lettering. For this exercise you will just write the alphabet as many times as will fit in the space provided. Looking back at the samples shown in this chapter, try to imitate 2 or 3 of them, put a star (★) by the style you like best.

~blank page~

NAME_____ DATE_____

Exercise 3-20

Practice Architectural Lettering

Transcribe the paragraph below while applying some of the concepts discussed previously in this chapter; your lettering should all be uppercase.

> A green roof is one which has vegetation growing on it. The value in this type of design is multi-fold. First, the roof reduces the load on the storm water system as the rain water is mostly retained on the roof to "feed" the vegetation. Second, the structure does not absorb as much solar radiation, thus requiring less energy to cool the building. Next, the green roof provides for insect and bird life which would otherwise be displaced by a new structure. It should be pointed out that a green roof weighs more than a traditional roof and thus requires a stronger building structure and during drought-like weather the vegetation needs to be irrigated – both of these things cost more but are often outweighed by the savings derived from the benefits previously mentioned.

Chapter 3 **EXERCISES**

~blank page~

NAME_____ DATE_____

Self-Exam:

The following questions can be used as a way to check your knowledge of this lesson. The answers can be found at the lower left on this page.

1.   Adding people to your sketches gives them a sense of scale and life. (T/F)

2.   Architects like to cross their corners when sketching. (T/F)

3.   The natural "arc" of the hand aids in drawing horizontal lines. (T/F)

4.   The _____ is the beginning of all architectural drawing.

5.   _____ drawing involves drawing with quick playful lines.

Review Questions:

The following questions may be assigned by your instructor as a way to assess your knowledge of this section. Your instructor has the answers to the review questions.

1.   The art of sketching is a learned talent. (T/F)

2.   Hatching is a technique used to represent doors. (T/F)

3.   Hand lettering is mostly uppercase in architectural drawings. (T/F)

4.   A vertical line is generally easier to draw than a horizontal line. (T/F)

5.   Computer text is sometimes added to scanned sketches. (T/F)

6.   _____ lines are often used for contrast in a sketch.

7.   Designers always write very neat letters. (T/F)

8.   Did you remember to add your name to the top of this page? (Y/N)

~blank page~

Formulating Design Solutions I

In this chapter we will talk about the design process used to formulate design solutions. Before the first line is drawn, the designer needs to collect sufficient data in order to make meaningful decisions. The focus of this book is drawing so we will not get too deep into the technical stuff.

The start of many *commissions* (i.e., a design job where you get paid) begin with a person's desire to start or grow a business, or a family wishing to remodel, expand or build a new home. At some point, using one of a variety of methods, they hire a designer to help them realize their vision. Once a contract is signed, the designer (or design team) can begin meeting with the Client to collect data about the project.

Another important preliminary step is to analyze the property on which the building will be built; the designer can determine the maximum buildable area based on local zoning ordinances and building codes.

Once a sufficient amount of data is collected and the site has been considered, the designer can begin to develop design solutions using the type of quick sketch studies covered in the previous chapter. Sometimes the designer will go through hundreds of design iterations in an attempt to fit the pieces of the puzzle together just right. A good designer will develop a solution that complies with government regulations, the client's requirements, is aesthetically pleasing and is technically sound (i.e., it keeps the rain, wind and snow out!).

To recap, the list below highlights many of the things a designer must factor into their design in order to reach an adequate solution:

1. Client Requirements
   a. Budget
   b. Program (more on this later)
   c. Timeline
   d. Sustainability
   e. Aesthetics
2. Government Regulations
   a. Zoning ordinances
   b. Local Building Codes
   c. State Building Codes
   d. National Building Codes
3. Climatic Conditions
   a. Hot/Freezing
   b. Rural/Urban
   c. Valley/Mountains
4. Site Conditions
   a. Wetlands
   b. Rivers/Lakes
   c. Ledge Rock
   d. Soil (clay, sandy, etc.)
5. Political/Cultural

A section of code books in an architectural office

The Program Statement

One of the first things a designer, or design team, does is to meet with the client and develop a *Program Statement*. A program statement is such an important step in the design process, it is almost hard to put into words. This document reveals the pieces to

the puzzle needed by the designer before they can begin sketching the first lines. This document is derived by one or more meetings between the designer and the client, where many questions are asked about the spaces needed, what will be happening in these spaces and when. The client typically has a pretty good idea about what spaces are needed – for example, one might say "I need three offices, one for each of my sales people". Additionally, the designer's experience and knowledge of the various building codes will reveal other rooms required like recycling rooms, toilet rooms, mechanical and electrical rooms.

In addition to the function and number of rooms, the ideal square footage for each room is specified. These numbers might come from the client, whose intimate knowledge of the business helps select the size, or from the designer, who may have designed previous buildings of the type under consideration.

In the end, a document is created (see the example on the next page) that lists each room and its ideal size. This document can then be used to put together preliminary construction costs and design fees. If the client's budget is sufficient, then the project can move forward, and the designer has a firm understanding of the client's needs.

Sometimes the *Program Statement* includes an **Adjacency Matrix**. This matrix is used to dictate when one room needs to be close to another room. For example, in a hospital project, the Emergency Room needs to be close, if not connected, to the X-ray department so patients are not traveling great distances. Conversely, some rooms may need to be separated by a great distance; for example, a music recording studio wants to be remote from the mechanical room or any other noise producing spaces.

On the next page you will find an example of a project program that acts as a preliminary design tool – which forms the puzzle pieces – when laying out a floor plan.

The next section in this chapter begins a dialogue on sketching charts and diagrams. The conclusion of this discussion talks about Bubble and Block Diagrams – the information from this program is used to create the "bubbles" and "blocks" used in those diagrams.

Sketch by **Alan Anderson**; Duluth, MN

STEEL CITY COMMUNITY CENTER
Architectural Program

Common Spaces	*Total SF*
Welcome Area (Waiting/Reception)	400
Multi-Purpose Room	900
Public Restrooms (Adult/Child)	300
Staff Lounge	100
* Kitchen	200
Maintenance - Storage	100
Sub-Total	2,000

Shared ECFE and Pre-School Spaces	*Total SF*
Shared Meeting Room	400
Resource Area/Book and Toy Library	300
* Classroom Equipment Storage	300
Staff Office Space	500
Interview/Conference Rooms (2 @ 100 SF each)	200
Staff Resource - Work Room	150
Sub-Total	1,850

Steel City School District	*Total SF*
Preschool Classrooms (2 @ 800 SF each)	1,600
Preschool Classroom	1,000
Parent Room	500
Sub-Total	3,100

Pre-School	*Total SF*
Preschool Classrooms (2 @ 900 SF each)	1,800
Sub-Total	1,800

Oakey County - Adult/Family Services	*Total SF*
Waiting	150
Reception/Office (2 workstations)	150
Counselor Offices (3 @ 100 SF each)	300
* Basic Education Classroom	800
Fuel Assistance/Foodshelf Office (2 workstations)	150
Foodshelf	400
Loading Dock	150
Weatherization Office	100
Weatherization Work Room	150
Sub-Total	2,350

Total Assignable Area (80%)	**11,100**
Total Non-Assignable (20%)	**2,775**
Total Gross Area (100%)	**13,875**

* Negotiable areas (i.e., first to be cut in size or out of program).

Site Development	Total SF
Parking (60 cars plus school bus drop-off)	12,000
Playground	1,000
Service/Delivery @ Loading Dock	1,000
Total	14,000

A few comments will be made about the program statement before moving on. The types and number of rooms are clearly identified and the desired size is also listed. All of the desired spaces are referred to as "assignable area" in contrast to "non-assignable area" which accounts for required spaces such as mechanical rooms, electrical and data rooms.

In addition to specific building elements, the site development has its major features mentioned so they can be considered in early design concepts. For example, maybe the multi-purpose room should be near the playground.

As the project proceeds, the design team will revisit the program statement and add a column showing the actual square footage. It is not practical to expect the design would ever achieve 100% square footage compliance with the program, but each room should be within an agreed upon percentage (e.g., 5-10%).

The sketch below does not relate to the discussion at hand, but is provided in an attempt to fill whitespace in the book with "inspirational" drawings. Enjoy!

Sketch by Steve **McNeill**

Diagrams

We are all familiar with typical diagrams of everyday life, such as the *Pie Diagram*, the *Graph* and the *Bar Chart* as shown below. You see these diagrams in newspapers, magazines, science books and computer programs like *Microsoft Excel* and *Quicken* (by Intuit). These basic diagrams aid in dissecting and disseminating information. Architectural designers also use these types of diagrams in their practice. Here you will take a look at how this fundamental concept can be used within the context of sketching to break down large chunks of information to aid in the decision/design process.

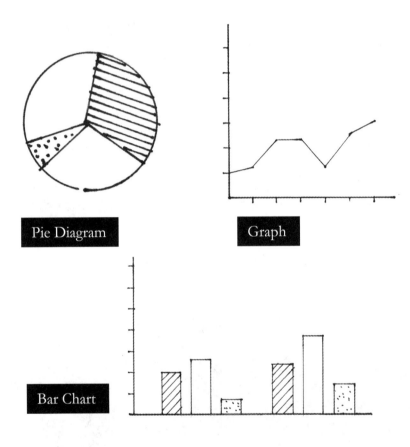

Pie Diagram

Graph

Bar Chart

Your skills with these diagrams, or proto drawings as we refer to them, can enable you to express ideas pictorially, define decisions and even organize large complex tasks such as reports, term papers and drawing presentations

Project Storyboard

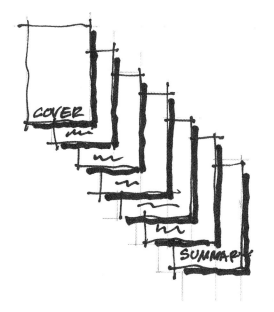

We often find that *Reports*, *Proposals* and *Text* documents can be organized as shown in the image to the left.

Note each element or area has a title which describes, and represents, a portion of work that must be done to complete a project.

When shared with staff, this Project Storyboard helps people to focus on the elements rather than feel overwhelmed by the project as a whole.

Each element above may in fact be complex in and of itself, and thus may need to be broken down further. For example, each section above could represent the work required by the various disciplines on a specific project: Architectural, Structural, Mechanical, Electrical, Civil, Food Service Consultant, Fire Protection, etc. Thus, each section is analyzed and diagramed to indicate the various tasks required by each discipline in order to complete the project.

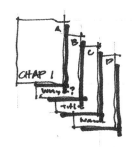
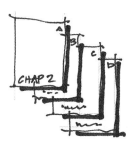
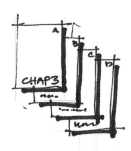

When considering the pages in a book (such as this one) or in a school report, you may use storyboarding to visualize the information you think will fit on each page. This will help you determine how many pages are needed overall and how best to divide up the work when working in a group. These images may be as small as the one shown to the left or may be a full-size page.

Storyboards are very useful in the planning of *Plan Sets* or *Drawing Presentations*. The sheets required can be piled up or tiled (see both examples below).

The first example below graphically lists each sheet and a label is added. This would be a breakdown for boards needed for a presentation or a very early preliminary "stab" at the number of drawings needed for a set of Construction Drawings (the set of drawings the contractor bids and builds from). The designer could sketch this in a sketch book or on 8½″ x 11″ bond paper (copy machine paper).

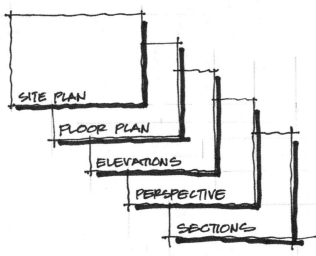

Not only is a sheet study useful for dividing up the work for your staff, but it is also used to determine the amount of time required to complete the project. Many designers use past projects to determine the average amount of time needed to complete one sheet. Therefore, when calculating the time needed to do a new project, a storyboard can be used – taking the number of sheets multiplied by the hours needed per sheet (so: 6 sheets X 40 hours = 240 hours).

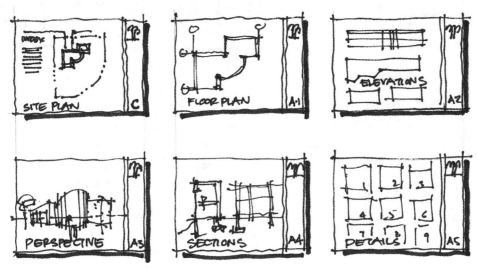

The *Sheet Storyboard* (which some like to refer to as the *Cartoon Set*) requires a certain amount of experience to know which drawings and details would be needed on any given project type. Additionally, the approximate amount of space required by each drawing can be hard to know for sure, so more or fewer sheets may be required and should be taken into consideration (especially when using this method to calculate fees and budgets).

So you might be thinking to yourself, why not just list the project components in a check list? Well, for some reason the visual process seems very effective for teams as well as the individual in adding clarity to the task at hand; designer-types often think better visually whereas engineers like to use lists more. These little pictures, storyboards, or vignettes are very powerful! Not to mention, if a potential employer sees a few examples of this in your portfolio (*i.e., examples of your work*) they will think it's cool and hire you (well, maybe – but it sure can't hurt).

Decision Tree

Architectural practice involves, more than anything, getting decisions on where, what, how and how much to build. A very useful "thinking diagram" that clarifies visually much talk and discussion is the *Decision Tree*. There are many types of decision trees, but the basics are covered here.

TIP: Get in the habit of putting shadows on your boxes (i.e., the heavy dark line on two sides) to make them "pop" off the page.

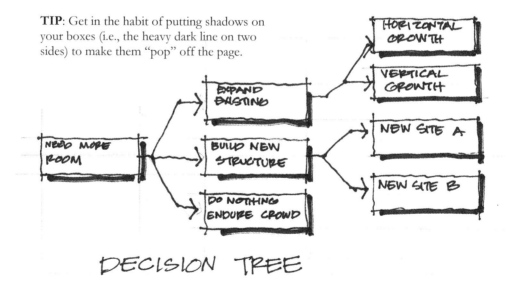

The example on the previous page shows the analysis of a problem – a business or home owner "needing more room". Given that problem, they have at least three options: *1)* Expand their existing facilities; *2)* Build a New Building; *3)* Do nothing and live with the inconvenience and lost revenue. From those three options, each then has its own set of options – for example: within the context of expanding, one could expand vertically (add additional floor) or horizontally (if the site was large enough). As you can imagine, this could go on and on until the utmost detail was revealed about each possible option, including timelines, costs, risks and rewards. The final result is the ability to make an informed decision.

The *Decision Tree* can be combined with small diagrams and sketches to almost instantly portray options. This type of sketching can often be done right in front of the client, utilizing the knowledge of both the designer (knowing codes and construction issues) and the client (knowing budgets and timelines), with an economy of time!

The drawing below shows the same Decision Tree as the one on the previous page, but with sketches rather than words. Assuming enough preliminary information exists to create the sketches shown below, then you can see how much more revealing this Decision Tree would be compared to the one on the previous page.

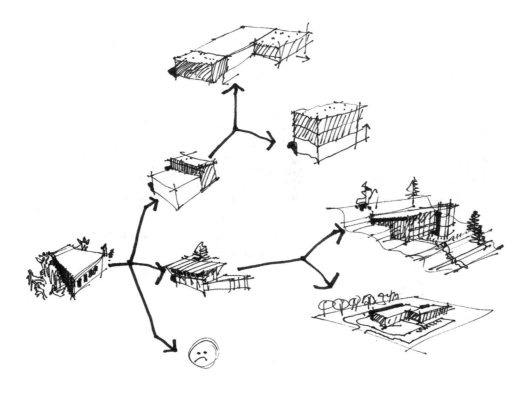

Circulation Diagrams

Buildings are largely composed of two basic functions: 1) *Activity Areas* such as living rooms, offices, cafeterias, etc., and 2) *Circulation Areas* such as hallways, corridors, lobbies and exit passages. It is often necessary to analyze the "paths" people follow to get from one space to another in an effort to determine if the path is efficient (e.g., distance) and unobstructed (e.g., not crossing other paths) – this can be done with a *Circulation Diagram*.

A building's circulation areas can be simple or complex. In either case it is possible to study the flow as "piping", "networks" or "vessels" similar to our veins and arteries. These circulation areas are often diagramed using width to indicate volume, as shown in the diagram below. As people exit the corridor (for example, they enter a room) the "load" on the corridor is reduced and as people enter the same corridor (for example, a hallway connects to it) the "load" increases. So, at some point the corridor may need to be very wide at the heaviest load, but as the load dwindles (usually at the extremities) there may be an opportunity to make the corridor narrower, allowing more space for the adjacent rooms or even reducing the size of the building.

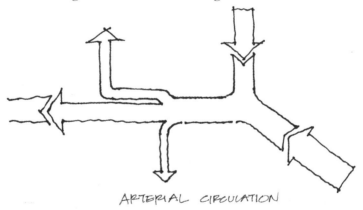

ARTERIAL CIRCULATION

The above example is a sketch of a linear circulation diagram and a closed loop diagram is shown below.

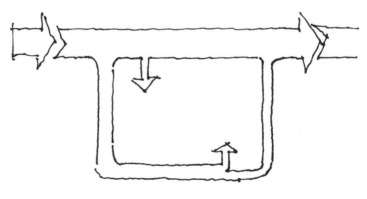

LOOP OR NETWORK CIRCULATION

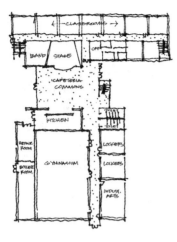

Now you will take a more realistic example of a Circulation Diagram, using the school building floor plan shown to the left. A quick look at the plans reveals the following components: the north (i.e., top) block contains the classrooms and offices, the center area houses the cafeteria/auditorium with an adjacent kitchen, while the south portion contains the gymnasium and locker rooms.

In both images on this page, the circulation areas are *Hatched* with a *Stipple* pattern (which is a series of random dots made with the tip of a pen or pencil).

In the floor plan below the circulation diagram reveals the path students would travel from the classrooms to the cafeteria and then to the playground and finally back to the classrooms. Notice how the diagram lines start out narrow and then get thicker as the students converge near the center. The overall circulation is fairly smooth but it is revealed that the toilet rooms are in a rather inconvenient location which may discourage students from washing their hands before eating!

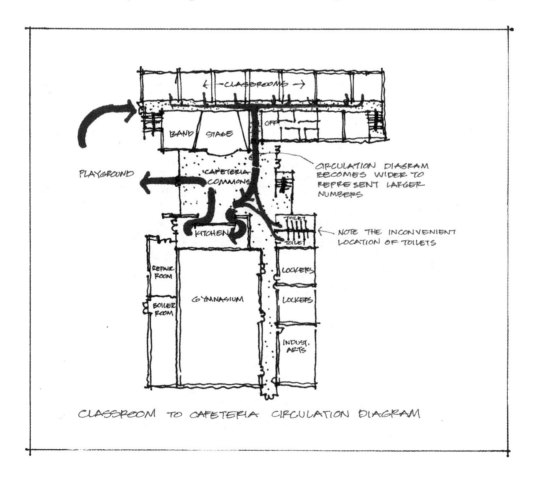

It may have surprised you that the designer is concerned about whether a student washes his hands or not, but this is a good example of the subtle effects the built environment can have on its occupants; not only circulation, but equipment noise, natural daylight, air quality and finishes.

Now let's consider the same school building and diagram the circulation for a situation where large numbers of students are released to lunch from both the classrooms and the gymnasium area at the same time. As you can see, things get pretty messy as paths cross and the students coming from the classrooms are even less likely to wash their hands now that another obstacle has been put in their way, that is, a large and hungry group of students!

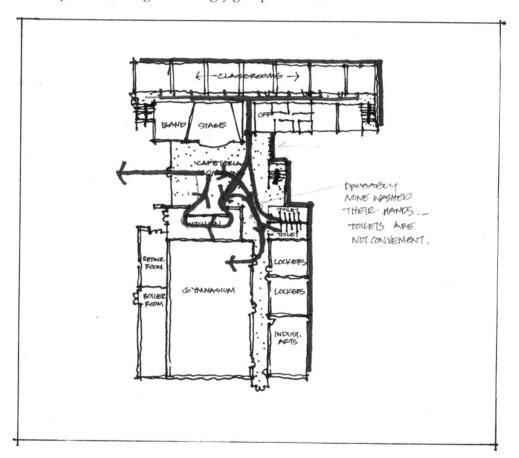

Circulation diagrams are also used to verify building codes are complied with – which require a certain number of exits and widths based on several factors. The authors often work in one State which required a plan diagram to be submitted.

In conclusion, the Circulation Diagram might reveal the need to develop another design solution. Maybe another bank of toilets can be added near the classroom, or it might be that the entire floor plan needs to be revisited. Another outcome might relate to the building's operations, where the client makes the decision to offset the time when the students are released from the classrooms and the gym.

Notes:

NAME_____DATE_____

Exercise 4-1

Storyboard Exercise – Data
Take a report or similar document and diagram it into sub-components; break the information into bite sized chunks. If you are at a loss, diagram your daily class schedule or this textbook. Do your work in the empty square below.

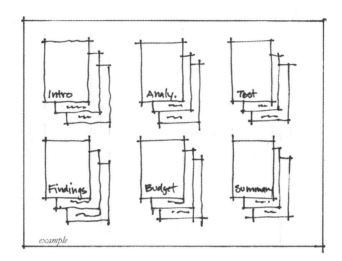

~blank page~

NAME_____ DATE_____

Exercise 4-2

Storyboard Exercise – Drawing Set

Using the information you learned in this chapter, create a Storyboard (or Cartoon Set) to show approximately how many sheets would be needed to document the existing conditions of the building pictured below (i.e., a Record Set). Assume the building is symmetrical, the floor plan will fit on one sheet and two of the four elevations will fit on a sheet. Try to represent the building shapes.

~blank page~

NAME_____ DATE_____

Exercise 4-3

Decision Tree
Create a decision tree for an event, perhaps an important event such as a wedding or a trip. Pick something with lots of options. Use the back side of this page if you need more space. Make a small "+" or "-" below each option to indicate a good option versus a bad option. Place a star by each decision you actually made (or would make if you where to do this thing). The stars will identify a "path" taken or to be taken.

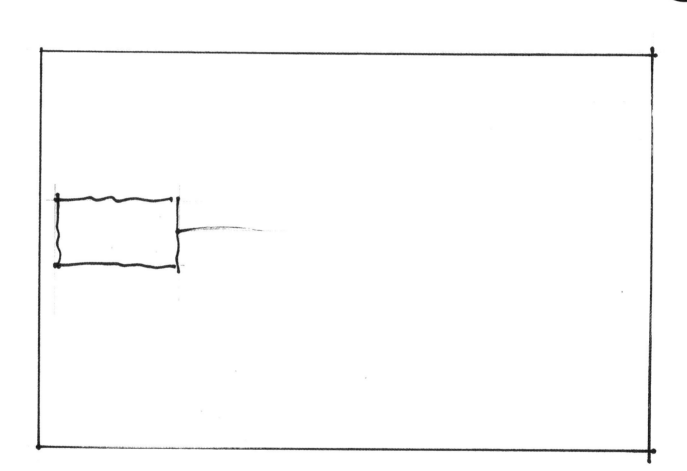

~blank page~

NAME_____DATE_____

Exercise 4-4

Pictorial Decision Tree

In this exercise you will create a decision tree using graphics to represent a decision (e.g., sketch an air plane to represent flying to a location). Use the decision from the previous exercise for this exercise. Make sure you get all the decisions along the prefered (or starred) path. Add as many of the other decisions as possible after that.

~blank page~

NAME_____ DATE_____

Exercise 4-5

Circulation Diagram

Create a circulation diagram showing student "flow" from the gymnasium to the Locker rooms (for both male and female students) and then back to the classrooms (classrooms are located on both the first and second floors). Try using a colored pen or felt tipped pen if you have one.

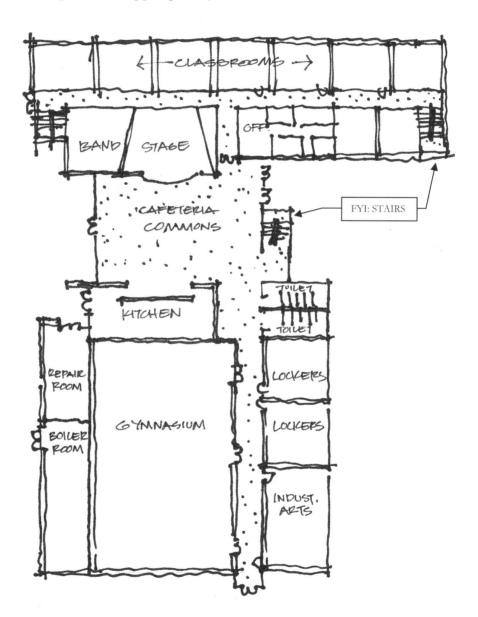

~blank page~

NAME_____ DATE_____

Chapter 4 Questions

Self-Exam:
The following questions can be used as a way to check your knowledge of this lesson. The answers can be found at the lower left on this page.

1. *Cartoon Sets* can be used to determine how much time will be needed to design a building. (T/F)

2. An *Adjacency Matrix* lists nearby buildings. (T/F)

3. *Diagrams* can be used to break down large chunks of data. (T/F)

4. A _____ diagram shows how people move around in a building.

5. When drawing boxes in diagrams, what helps them "pop" off the page?

    _____.

Review Questions:
The following questions may be assigned by your instructor as a way to assess your knowledge of this section. Your instructor has the answers to the review questions.

1. A *Program Statement* is an important part of the design process. (T/F)

2. The *Decision Tree* is mainly used by architects to determine which type of pencil to draw with. (T/F)

3. A *Commission* is a job in which you are paid. (T/F)

4. What is collected from a client at the beginning of a project: _____.

5. A _____ _____ lists the rooms needed.

6. *Project Storyboards* are useful in the planning of plan sets. (T/F)

7. Complex problems are made more manageable via *Diagrams*. (T/F)

8. An experienced designer can approximate how many sheets will be needed in a drawing set by creating a *Cartoon Set*. (T/F)

~blank page~

Chapter

5

Formulating Design Solutions II

With most of the "facts" about the desired building in hand, the designer (or better, design team) can begin developing drawings.

The design process is very much a team effort where many talents are brought together in order to derive the best design solution possible. Architecture is often depicted in movies as an individual feat, when in fact many people are involved even on the smallest of projects. When an arrogant attitude is taken, the design suffers. Therefore, design teams often have group meetings to talk about progress and challenges so decisions can be made quicker; the photo below depicts one such meeting.

Design team meeting in large, open, and naturally lit space with a marker-board type wall.

Concept Diagrams

With most of the puzzle pieces in hand (program, site, etc.), the designer can generate a *Concept Diagram* which is meant to convey the project's "big idea". Below is an example of a concept drawing for a new office complex at a manufacturing facility. The elements are simple shapes that do not have to relate to the actual shape of the building. (In fact, that is not usually even known at this stage of the design.) Again, you may think of these as the major pieces to the puzzle, with this sketch being used as a visual thinking exercise. This kind of drawing may be created in front of the design team and/or the client.

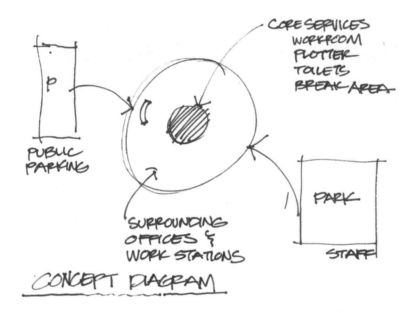

Form Diagrams

The *Form Diagram* is an example of small thumbnail sketches meant to study the basic shapes and proportions the building could take. Looking at the image on the next page, we have taken the *Concept Diagram* (from above) and further developed it into this new drawing (the Form Diagram) – which looks at the impact of the various design goals such as elongation in the East-West direction; lots of exterior skin for windows, but a simple rectangular composition which allows daylight to reach deep into the building. Also, the intent to try and locate much of the "core" components near the center of the building is shown. The "core" components might be spaces such as toilet rooms, mechanical rooms, and other rooms that do not required natural light; thereby placing more of the occupied spaces directly on an exterior wall and in line with natural lighting – which reduces lighting loads/costs and makes the space more enjoyable for its occupants.

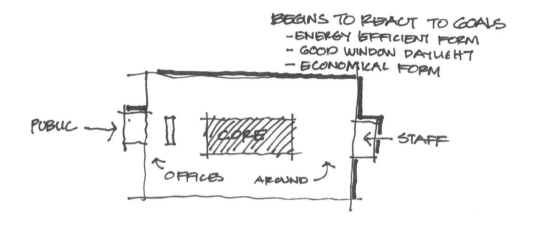

FORM DIAGRAM 1

The next iteration of the Form Diagram takes the ideas developed above and slightly modifies them as shown in the image below. Not every sketch needs to be a completely "ingenious" new idea – a few may be, but not all will be. The best design solution is often found by trying many options and refining them as problems arise or new information comes to light. Notes are added to help recall how this diagram was achieved, which is really helpful when you are going back through 20-30 options and wonder how you got to that point originally. The notes added should be simple statements identifying what is different about that sketch from the previous one. Finally, notice how heavy black lines on two common sides suggest a shadow and give the sketch a sense of three dimensions.

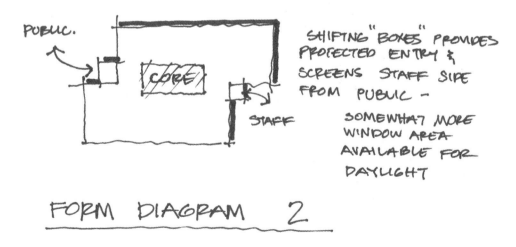

FORM DIAGRAM 2

Further "branching" of ideas often leads to a consideration of the growth options for a given design. Is there an option that allows for growth for the given design that also fits on the site? After studying a few options, is one found that looks less like an addition with minimal impact to adjacent areas when considering circulation and day lighting? This future growth study may reveal that the site is inadequate for a client's long term growth and another location should be found on which to build, or maybe the building's structure needs to be designed to support additional floors.

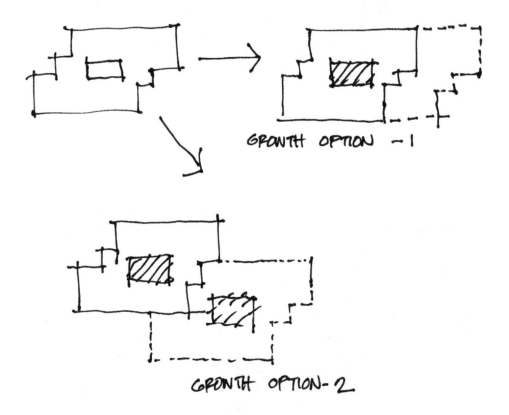

GROWTH OPTION — 1

GROWTH OPTION — 2

At this point, none of these sketches need to be to scale (meaning you should not expect to place a ruler or scale on the drawing to see how big the building is). You will have to validate these very preliminary options later in conjunction with the *Program*. Here you are just playing around with ideas in your sketchbook based on early information collected.

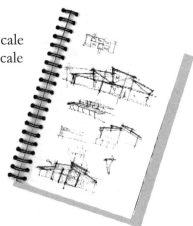

Thumbnail Diagram

The *Thumbnail Diagram* can be set down onto the paper as if in perspective (the process of drawing in perspective will be covered in detail later in the book). The example below is similar to a *Decision Tree* diagram discussed earlier, but here you are starting from a "decided" point on that decision tree. Notice the upper-left potion of the image below represents the outline of the second Form Diagram on the previous page. With a specific form in mind, you can extend construction "rays" up from the corners and depict the basic box (again, more on the specifics later on in the book).

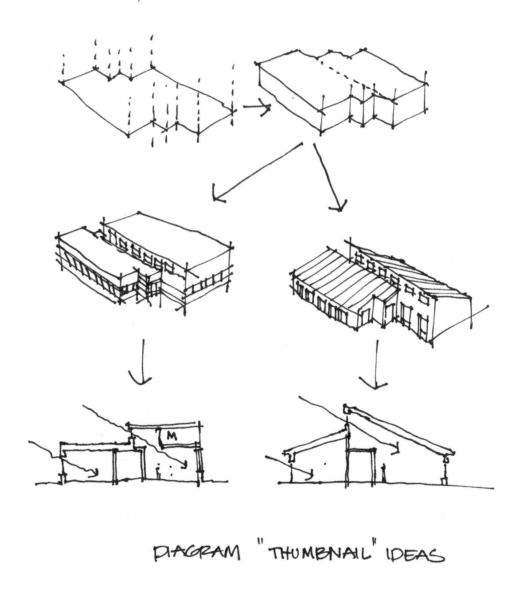

DIAGRAM "THUMBNAIL" IDEAS

The basic "massing" form can be used as an "underlay" and then branched out into two very different building forms for consideration. Each form has a unique cross-section which is sketched below each option to start to think about the structure and to illustrate how the sun's rays penetrate into the building through window openings.

Note that these are quick *Sketch Book* ideas, but if you were to enlarge them on a photocopier and post them on a wall, they could act as your "thinking storyboard" of how this design came to be. Some firms have what are called *Design Critiques* which allow the larger design team, or colleagues, to hear about your design and to challenge certain decisions or draw out certain issues not previously considered. These *Thumbnail Diagrams* are perfect for the early design critique process.

Building Section Thumbnail Diagram

In addition to the building section concept just introduced on the previous page (which looked generically at volumes and not so much at constructability), thumbnail sketches often study what is happening with the structure in a building section. The sketches below are abstract diagrams, in that they are only showing the structural components of the building (i.e., the roof beams, columns and footings), which omit the architectural elements such as the walls and roof. A sketch like this opens up discussions of economy and flexibility. Little stick figures are added to suggest the scale of the structure. This type of analysis would likely be done in conjunction with a Structural Engineer, who is ultimately responsible for the structural design.

3 BAY STRUCTURE
MORE COLUMNS / LESS FLEXIBLE

2 BAY STRUCTURE
- MORE FLEXIBLE / MORE COST

BUILDING SECTION STUDY

Light/Sun Ray Diagram

Architecture for many of us is, at its simplest, a manipulation of light and space. A cross section study that analyzes the sun's path is frequently done to study how well lit, or not, the space may be.

This sketch applies the rule-of-thumb which says good daylight of space can occur up to 2½ times the height of the window opening. The diagonal line shown is what we will refer to as the *Sun Ray Line*.

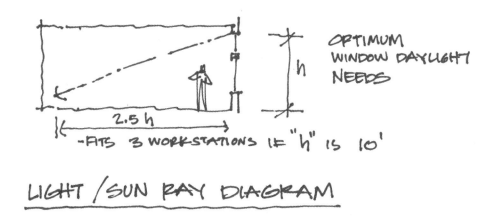

Below is a section generated as part of a real design process. This early sketch begins to reveal the thickness of building elements like walls, floors and the roof. The structure is loosely implied and minimal information is added (for internal use only, e.g., the roof slope and light ray data).

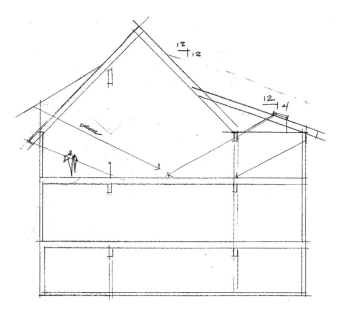

Bubble Diagram

The *Bubble Diagram* is probably one of the most used diagrams in the Architectural Profession when it comes to design layout of a building. It is a quick way to start thinking about where various rooms should go in a building. As you can imagine, a circle is quicker to draw than a square or rectangular shape – no corners!

The circles are not so much to scale as they are proportionally correct relative to each other. So if a Living room needed to be 800sf and a Dining room 400sf, your circle for the living room would be twice the size of the dining room. All the circles should be labeled so you can refer back to them later and make sense of them.

Arrows can also be added, as shown in the sketch below, to indicate relationships of circulation. So an arrow connecting two spaces (i.e., circles) may indicate the two spaces need to be near each other (like the mudroom and the garage), or it may indicate a desire to walk from one room directly into another (by a door or opening in the wall between the two rooms). This is helpful when you are trying several options; you may be tempted to move a room that should be near another room that you were not planning to move, which would create a problem.

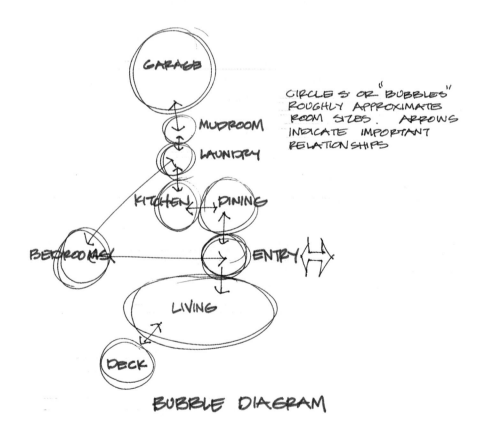

Block Diagram

The *Block Diagram* is different from the previously covered *Form Diagram* in that the Block Diagram deals with individual spaces and the Form Diagram entire buildings. This type of diagram is the next step from the *Bubble Diagram.*

This is a great diagrammatic drawing to show the client and get their initial impression, because 1) it does not take too much time so if big changes are needed it will not be a problem, and 2) the client will not think the drawing is done and won't be afraid to request changes. A computer drawn plan loaded with dimensions would give the impression that the drawings are set in stone and cannot be changed, causing the client to possibly compromise on a change that otherwise might not have been a problem.

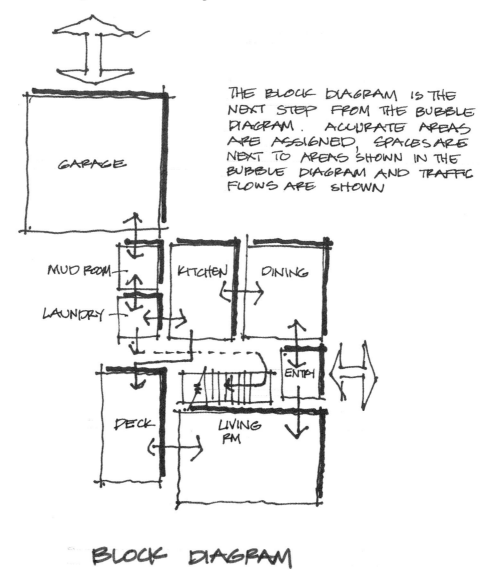

THE BLOCK DIAGRAM IS THE NEXT STEP FROM THE BUBBLE DIAGRAM. ACCURATE AREAS ARE ASSIGNED, SPACES ARE NEXT TO AREAS SHOWN IN THE BUBBLE DIAGRAM AND TRAFFIC FLOWS ARE SHOWN

BLOCK DIAGRAM

The drawing below is the result of an overlay sketch based on the *Block Diagram* shown on the previous page. Some would prefer to show a drawing like this to a client rather than the more abstract sketch shown on the previous page – it really comes down to preference. On larger projects where there are more client meetings, you may show both: the Block Diagram at an earlier meeting and then this loosely sketched floor plan at a follow up meeting.

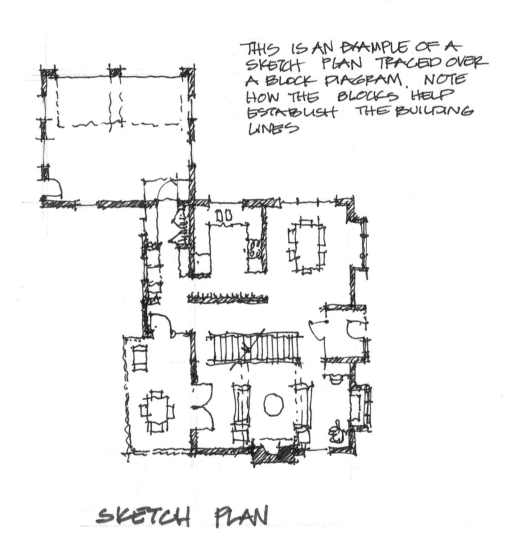

THIS IS AN EXAMPLE OF A SKETCH PLAN TRACED OVER A BLOCK DIAGRAM. NOTE HOW THE BLOCKS HELP ESTABLISH THE BUILDING LINES

SKETCH PLAN

Tracing Paper

A favorite "tool" in the architectural designer's toolbox is *Tracing Paper*, which is also referred to as Bum-Wad. Tracing paper is a quick and easy way to clean up a drawing or start another design option based on a previous option; this would be a design iteration. Tracing paper is very lightweight and easy to see through, which makes tracing the page below it easy. If you did not have tracing paper, you would need to use a light table, which many designers have, but is usually inconveniently away from their desk as it is shared by the office.)

Tracing paper is available in two forms: by the sheet or on a roll. Most designers use tracing paper from a roll, often having a handful of roll widths on hand. The nice thing about a roll is that you are able to tear off a piece of paper of any length that you need. This is especially useful when working on two-point perspectives (covered in an upcoming chapter) and your vanishing points are widely spaced. The final sketch-over can then be done on a smaller piece of sketching paper (or higher quality paper) where the actually vanishing points do not need to appear.

The image below shows the tracing paper concept using the sketches from the two previous pages. It is handy to use drafting tape to hold the various overlays into place to keep them from moving around.

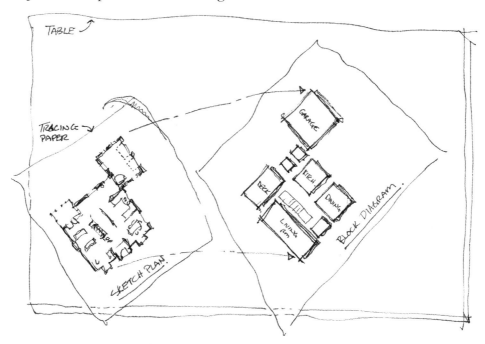

Site Planning

Preliminary site planning is typically done via hand sketching in order to look at several options quickly. Often these early sketches will be based on a survey drawing prepared in a CAD program; this will show the property lines, streets, existing buildings, utility locations (power, water, sewage, phone, cable, gas, etc.), and contours (which show the slope of the land).

A **Site Analysis Diagram** is an important step in understanding the land in which a building is be built. The building design should not even be started before this drawing has been done as it will determine where certain rooms should go and the location of windows. This diagram is also indispensible when considering "green" design options such as daylighting and passive solar design.

Looking at the sketch below, you can see several elements overlaid on the *Site Analysis Diagram*. A few of the items often found here are (in no particular order):

- Street Access
- Sun pattern
- Winter Wind direction
- Property lines

- Setbacks (code buildable area)
- Existing Trees
- True North
- Direction ground slopes

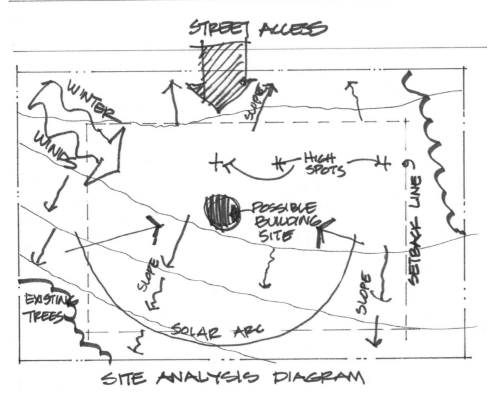

SITE ANALYSIS DIAGRAM

Actually determining sun angles and wind direction is beyond this book's scope.

Once the *Site Analysis Diagram* has been completed and the preliminary drawings for the building done, a **Basic Site Plan** can be drawn to show the client how the building will work on the site.

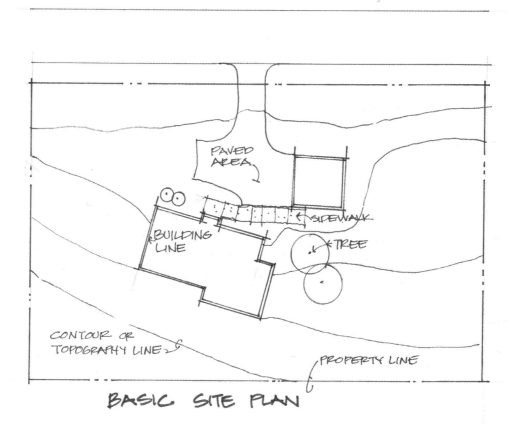

BASIC SITE PLAN

A few points about the graphics of the sketch above include:

- The buildings are just shown as outlines, no need to show interior walls. For larger, more complicated, buildings it is helpful to indicate where the exterior doors (both people doors and garage doors) are so the sidewalks and driveways can be properly located.

- Things are clearly labeled; property lines, paved areas, trees. Existing items, such as trees, roads, buildings, etc., should be labeled as such.

- New contours are shown (compare to sketch on previous page) to indicate how the rainwater will be dealt with as well as a rough idea about how much earthwork will be needed (i.e., cut and fill). This text is not meant to be a study in site design, but we will quickly mention that a good site design sheds rainwater away from any buildings (all sides) and tries to equalize the amount of cut and fill to minimize earthwork costs.

While the *Site Analysis Diagram* and the *Basic Site Plan* are shown to the client at meetings to determine if their needs are being met, a **Rendered Site Plan** is sometimes generated as a formal presentation to the owner/client, users and/or the public. The exact techniques on how a site plan is rendered can vary quite a bit. This type of sketch may be produced by the architect, a landscape architect, or a civil engineer depending on how the design team is structured.

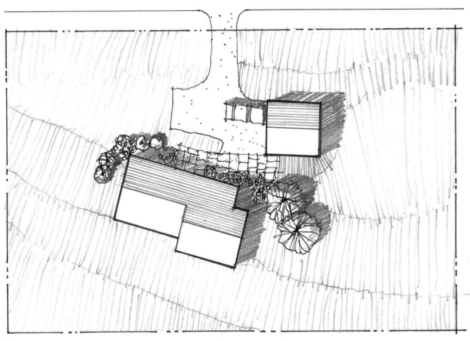

RENDERED SITE PLAN

Above is an example of a typical Rendered Site Plan. Its main features are:
- Lineweights to distinguish between materials and convey depth.
- Shadows to indicate solar impact at a specific time of year.
- Some surfaces/materials are hatched or highlighted; for example:
  - The roofing has parallel lines which usually indicate shingle roofing; and to distinguish between adjacent sloped surfaces one slope is often hatched differently (or not at all in this case) to make things more clear.
  - The paved driveway has a stipple hatch pattern, which is nothing more than several randomly placed dots.
  - The ground and its slope are highlighted by the light hatch pattern that runs continuous and perpendicular to the contours (water always flows perpendicular to the contours).

NAME_____ DATE_____

Exercise 5-1

Bubble Diagram
Quickly layout the floor plan using the various rooms provided below. Make sure each bubble is proportionately the correct size (relative to each other). Each space should be labeled. Note: the "bubbles" should all touch each other, as if their edges were common walls.

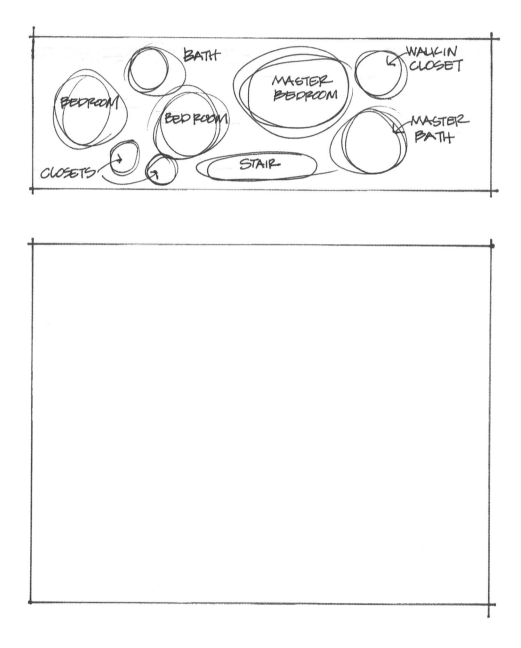

~blank page~

NAME_____ DATE_____

Exercise 5-2

Block Diagram

Use the "puzzle pieces" shown below to layout a second story floor plan of a single family home. Follow this mini-**program**: north is up, each bedroom must have windows, the south side has a lake view, provide minimal hallway space, and the master bedroom must have a view of the lake. Space between spaces implies circulation, i.e., hallways.

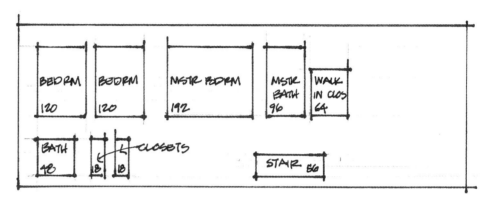

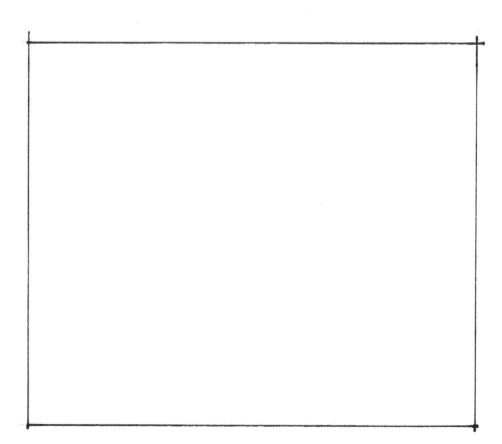

~blank page~

NAME_____ DATE_____

Exercise 5-3

Building Section Study
Analyze the photo below and develop a simple building section based on what you think is going on inside. Your section should cut through the middle (in the shorter direction) and through the tallest part. Show windows and doors in section if you are cutting though them. Do not worry about scale but try to be as proportionally correct as possible. Also, add the Sun Ray line.

~blank page~

NAME_____ DATE_____

Exercise 5-4

Building Section Study
This is a sketch of a New England village tavern, done with a felt tip pen and then a sepia Prismacolor® pencil over textured board. Draw a diagrammatic section through the "salt box" shaped tavern. Note that the tavern is built into a hill. Show the walkout level on the one side and the front porch (and street) on the other.

~blank page~

NAME_____ DATE_____

Exercise 5-5

Site Diagram

Take this house and garage and place them on the site plan shown below. Indicate the driveway from the road to the garage and also show sidewalks as needed. Use the graphic scale and notice the north direction. Add neat hand-written notes to label the house, garage, driveway and sidewalk.

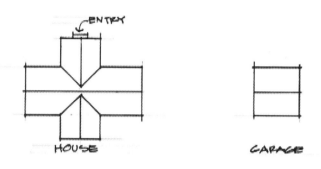

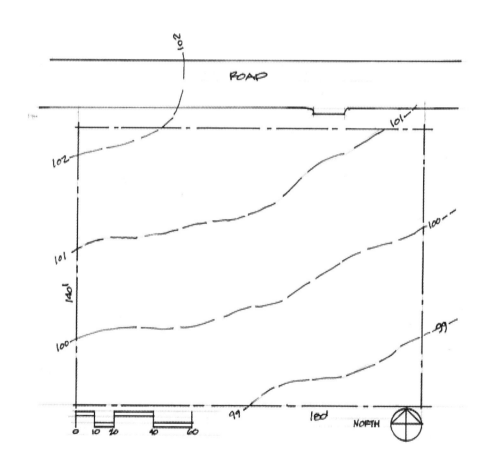

~blank page~

NAME_____ DATE_____

Self-Exam:
The following questions can be used as a way to check your knowledge of this lesson. The answers can be found at the lower left on this page.

1. Tracing paper is used for quick design iterations. (T/F)

2. A *Thumbnail Diagram* explores more refined options than does the *Form Diagram*. (T/F)

3. Ideally the site design will equalize the amount of cut and fill. (T/F)

4. A _____ diagram uses circles of various sizes (related to the *Program Statement*) to begin to layout the floor plan.

5. Which diagram conveys the project's "big idea"? _____.

Review Questions:
The following questions may be assigned by your instructor as a way to assess your knowledge of this section. Your instructor has the answers to the review questions.

1. The design process is a team effort (on most projects). (T/F)

2. Tracing paper is rarely needed as the first few sketches result in the best design solution. (T/F)

3. Every sketch should be an "ingenious" new idea. (T/F)

4. A *Rendered Site Plan* is often the first type of site plan drawn. (T/F)

5. Early design idea sketches and diagrams should always be to scale. (T/F)

6. A _____ _____ diagram reveals important information about the context in which the building will sit.

7. A *Building Section Diagram* can show how much _____ will be cast into a room through the windows.

8. The _____ diagram studies the proposed building's basic shapes and proportions.

9. A good site design sheds _____ away from the building.

10. A _____ diagram usually follows a *Bubble Diagram*.

~blank page~

Section Two
Intermediate Techniques

"Designs of purely arbitrary nature cannot be expected to last long".
Kenzo Tange 1913-2005

Still Life Drawing

Drawing freehand what you see with the eye can be a challenging, but rewarding, proposition. The exercise of drawing what you see is generally referred to as Still Life or Field Sketching. A still life could be a staged grouping of objects on a table or a grouping of buildings on a given portion of land.

When working on a sketch, the architectural designer has many techniques at his disposal. For example, there are steps one can take to quickly divide a line or a surface (i.e., one side of a 3D box) into equal segments or spaces. Additionally, a 3D drawing can be created that is actually to scale, meaning it can be accurately measured from, called an axonometric (covered in the next chapter). Even when sketching still life scenes or delineating shadows, the designer should be aware of a few fundamental concepts – and that is what this chapter is intended to show you.

Travel Sketches: *Vinland Bridge View* by **Duane Thorbeck** FAIA

Equally dividing a line...

Here is a tip for equally dividing a line... say you need eight equal spaces, such as the third line below. If you start at one end and try working your way to the other end you will almost never end up with equally spaced segments. (It is too hard to judge how big the segments should be.) The trick is to divide and conquer... start with one tick in the middle; it may not be perfect but you will get very close. Next, you can divide each half in half (see the second line below). You continue this process until you have the desired number of segments; this only works for even numbered segments.

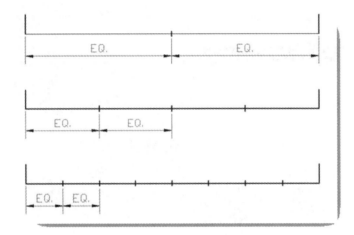

For odd numbered spacing, you use a scale or ruler. Find the number of spaces you want on the scale which is slightly larger than your line. And then position the first and last marks on the scale with the start and end of your line and project down as shown in the example below (the actual scale used does not matter).

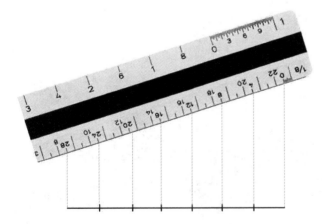

Dividing Spaces

When creating 2D or 3D drawings, you will often have the need to divide a previously created space or surface into smaller areas; for example, make a room in a floor plan exactly half its original size. As you will see in a moment, these methods apply to flat 2D surfaces as well as distorted surfaces which are part of a perspective drawing.

The following technique can be used to equally divide a space into equal pieces. You can, of course, repeat this process to even further divide a space already divided. The graphic below pretty much speaks for itself; you start with any rectilinear face (a simple square is shown here) and sketch an 'X' from which you can project lines from its center point. The center of the "X" is the center of the space in both directions.

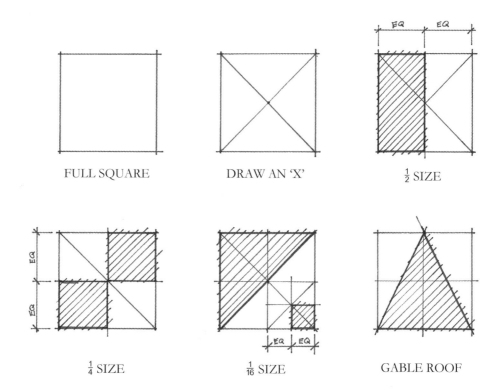

FULL SQUARE   DRAW AN 'X' $\frac{1}{2}$ SIZE

$\frac{1}{4}$ SIZE $\frac{1}{16}$ SIZE   GABLE ROOF

Drawing a Circle

In addition to previously drawn spaces (or squares), you may sketch a rectilinear area as a reference to aid in creating another shape. In a way, you can think of this process as if your square or rectangle were a chuck of wood and you are about to carve away to create another shape from the larger object. This next example uses most of what you learned on the previous page to create a [near perfect] circle. Designers who have been drawing for years are able to create a pretty good circle without this kind of help; however, they would still do it on a major building element that they wanted to be very accurate and maybe even symmetrical about the building façade.

The sketches below pretty much speak for themselves, but a brief outline will be provided to be sure you understand the concept.

1. Draw a square.
2. Draw an "X" to locate the center.
3. Add a horizontal line which passes through the center of the "X".
4. Add a vertical line which passes through the center of the "X".
5. Add two dots, as shown, to divide the diagonal line into three equal spaces.
6. Draw the circle.
   a. The horizontal and vertical lines locate the midpoints of the square – this corresponds to the four quadrants of a circle.
   b. The circle should past just outside the outermost dots on the diagonal lines

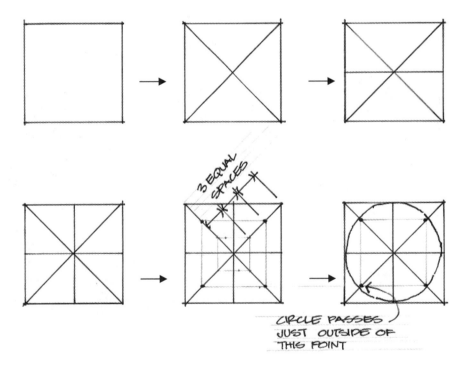

Dividing 3D Spaces

Below are examples of dividing a face and inscribing a circle on a three-dimensional object. The steps are identical to the steps outlined on the previous page; you start with the "X" and then add the vertical and horizontal lines. The top example is an isometric box and the bottom one is in perspective (you will learn more about this soon). The bottom example also shows how you can apply the same technique to multiple surfaces (the front and back in this case) and then connect the dots to develop a 3D object – a cylinder in this case! You will have an opportunity to try this on some pre-drawn 3D shapes in the exercise section of this chapter.

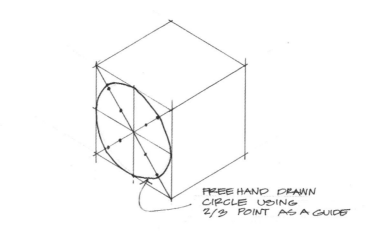

FREE HAND DRAWN
CIRCLE USING
2/3 POINT AS A GUIDE

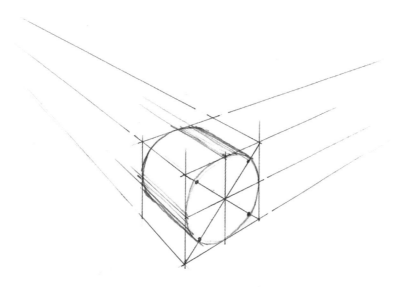

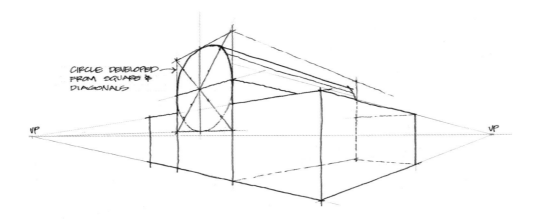

Taking what you just learned, plus some additional information you will be introduced to in the next chapter, you can easily sketch something such as the example shown above. This is a simple two point perspective started by developing basic rectilinear shapes and then breaking those shapes and surfaces down by dividing and inscribing a circular element as shown. The extra lines are then erased; or better yet, if you are using pen (which is preferred), you would create a more refined sketch using a tracing paper overlay as described in the previous chapter.

Still Life Drawing

There are many ways in which to learn and practice hand sketching architectural drawings. One quick and easy way is to use the *Still Life* technique; which involves using something in its natural state/setting or creating a prop of sorts as in the photo below. The interesting thing about the *Still Life* depicted in the photo below, it could just as easily be a group of buildings in a campus setting or an urban area.

The photo above, which will be used as the *Still Life* example for the following pages, was quickly erected using found items: blocks of wood, a coffee cup, an apple, and a chunk of pipe insulation. Notice how the natural daylight softens the shadows and makes them less distinct; using a flood light in a darker room will make the shadows more distinct and crisp, which would be easier to depict in a sketch.

It is possible to simply sit near the *Still Life* setting and sketch it, or it may be more convenient to snap a picture and work from that. You should never just trace over the photo (with tracing paper for example) unless you just plan on practicing hatching and adding shade and shadow.

Once you have your *Still Life* setup, and are ready to get started sketching, you may want to mentally divide the scene into quadrants. This will help you to lay things out with the proper proportions on the paper. This method is helpful to people new to *Still Life* sketching. However, experienced artists rarely do this; at least not on paper (rather in their mind). If you are working from a photo you could even mark the quadrant lines right on the photo.

Start your sketch, add the quadrant lines lightly and rough out the basics. Notice in the image below that the major reference lines and shapes have been laid down first. One major reference line is the angled line across the bottom, which will help to align the vertical block on the left and the flat on the right, as they align (or nearly align) as seen in the photo on the previous page. A circle for the apple has also been added.

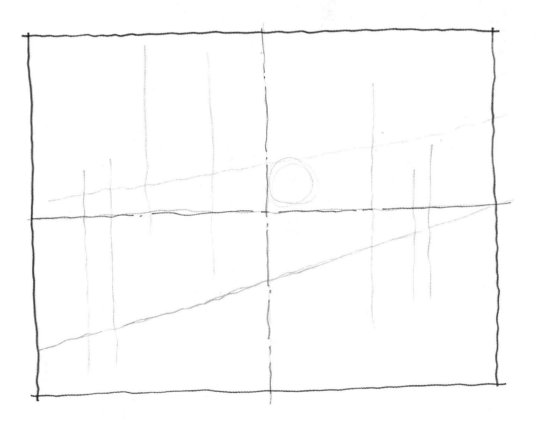

On the next page you can see an intermediate step and the end goal of a loosely sketched still life with shades and shadows added. At this point you are just practicing sketching what you see with your eyes, later in this book you will learn some of the mechanics behind what you see, which will help speed the process and result in more accurate sketches. So at this point (when you get to the exercises), work towards quick sketches in which you focus your energies on line quality.

Still Life sketching can be done with pretty much anything as the subject. As you can see in the sketches below, Architect Alan Anderson spent some time and drew these military jets from different angles.

Airplane sketches by **Alan Anderson**, Duluth, MN

Travel sketch by
Steve McNeill

The opportunities for *Still Life* sketching are endless. Below you see a more refined sketch with blended shades and shadows (using a blending stick or finger) created by a Certified Interior Designer while a student at the University of Wisconsin - Stout.

Still Life sketch by **Anne Porter CID**

Architectural Field Sketching

The idea of *Still Life* sketching can be "super sized" and applied to real-life architectural settings, which is referred to as *Field Sketching*. With this process, Architects can keep their sketching skills sharp – practicing eye-hand coordination, line weights, hatching, shades and shadows, reflections, entourage, etc. This only requires a pen and a sketch book!

Field sketch

To mix things up a little, try creating the same field sketch a few hours later, completely from memory! The image below is a *Memory Sketch*…

Memory sketch

NAME_____ DATE_____

Exercise 6-1

Dividing Spaces

Use the squares on the left and practice dividing them into smaller squares; make each one progressively smaller (i.e., 4, 16, 64). And then practice sketching circles in the other three squares.

Chapter 6   EXERCISES

~blank page~

NAME_____ DATE_____

Exercise 6-2

Dividing Spaces

Use the faces in perspective below and practice dividing them into four equal spaces. When finished, add a circle over the top of your previous work on this page.

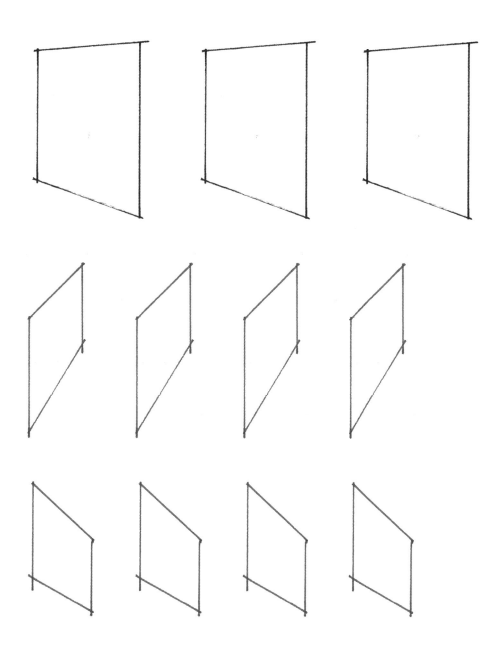

~blank page~

NAME_____DATE_____

Exercise 6-3

Dividing Spaces
Make two boxes ¼ of the original size, and two boxes ½ of the original size.
Then add a horizontal and a vertical cylinder to the last two boxes.

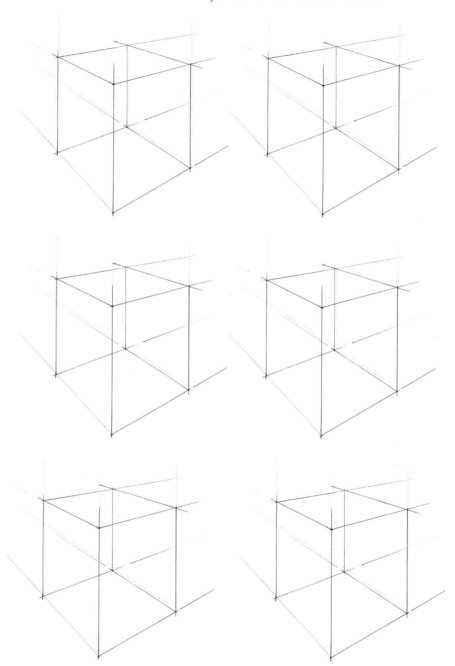

~blank page~

NAME_____ DATE_____

Exercise 6-4

Still Life

Sketch this still life using a pen or pencil. Do not use any straight edges for this exercise. Add the shade and shadows. You need not add the texture or imperfections of the block of wood.

~blank page~

NAME_____ DATE_____

Exercise 6-5

Still Life

Sketch this still life using a pen or pencil. Do not use any straight edges for this exercise. Add the shade and shadows. Do not add the texture or imperfections of the block of wood.

~blank page~

NAME_____ DATE_____

Exercise 6-6

Still Life

Sketch this still life using a pen or pencil. Do not use any straight edges for this exercise (not that is would help). Add the shade and shadows. Do not add the texture or imperfections of the apple.

~blank page~

NAME_____ DATE_____

Exercise 6-7

Still Life
Draw this still life; add the shades and shadows.

~blank page~

NAME_____ DATE_____

Self-Exam:
The following questions can be used as a way to check your knowledge of this lesson. The answers can be found at the lower left on this page.

1.   Drawing an "X" within a box aids in sketching a circle. (T/F)

2.   *Still Life Sketching* and *Field Sketching* are basically the same thing. (T/F)

3.   When dividing a line into an even number of equal spaces, you start in the middle and work your way out. (T/F)

4.   Whether dividing a rectangular space in half or into quadrants, you always start with an "X". (T/F)

5.   Some Architect's use _____ sketching, in a sketch book, to help keep their skills sharp.

Review Questions:
The following questions may be assigned by your instructor as a way to assess your knowledge of this section. Your instructor has the answers to the review questions.

1.   Field sketching involves mainly drawing farmsteads. (T/F)

2.   You draw an _____ to find the center of a box.

3.   Dividing a *Still Life* into quadrants helps with capturing proper proportions. (T/F)

4.   You can quickly throw together "found" items to create a *Still Life* scene. (T/F)

5.   You use a scale/ruler when dividing a line into uneven segments. (T/F)

6.   Drawing an "X" only helps to find the center of a flat 2D box and not a 3D surface. (T/F)

7.   Using a _____ _____ on a *Still Life* will sharpen shadows.

8.   Experienced artists always divide their *Still Life* into quadrants. (T/F)

9.   You can photograph a "scene" if on-site time is limited. (T/F)

10. The same technique is used to divide a line into both even and uneven segments. (T/F)

~blank page~

Self-Exam Answers:
1 – T, 2 – T, 3 – T, 4 – T, 5 – Field

~blank page~

Paraline Drawing

As you continue your journey in the study of creating architectural drawings, you will be introduced to the technique of creating isometric drawings as well as other drawing concepts that will help you create more accurate and more realistic looking drawings.

The process of drawing paraline drawings is more technical in practice than the perspective drawings you will learn to draw later in this book. The reason for this is that perspective drawings are often drawn freehand and are more "forgiving" when things are not quite right, whereas paraline drawings are composed of all parallel lines created with straightedge aids – such as triangles, T-Squares and parallel bars. The paraline drawing is also drawn to scale usually, so you also have to have an architectural scale handy and measure every line as you draw.

Paraline type images do not accurately depict reality – meaning you do not see the world around you in the way a paraline view is delineated. Rather, the view is intentionally distorted to simplify the drawing process and to allow the drawing to be scaled so that others can easily verify lengths and depths (say, for example, a contractor could measure an isometric drawing to determine the length of cabinets needed).

The drawing to the right is an isometric drawing rendered with marker which, in this example, has two *M. C. Escher* type distortions – college art class work.

Types of non-perspective 3D drawings

Below is a quick explanation of the various types of 3D drawings with the exception of perspective, which is covered in the next few chapters. Notice how the angles shown match the angles of the triangle tools introduced in chapter 1. (Of course, all vertical lines shown are drawn using the 90 degree side of a triangle.)

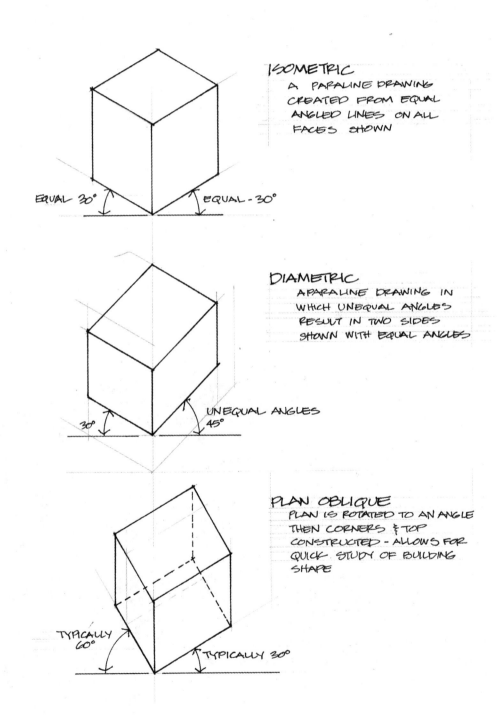

ISOMETRIC
A PARALINE DRAWING CREATED FROM EQUAL ANGLED LINES ON ALL FACES SHOWN

EQUAL 30°   EQUAL - 30°

DIAMETRIC
A PARALINE DRAWING IN WHICH UNEQUAL ANGLES RESULT IN TWO SIDES SHOWN WITH EQUAL ANGLES

UNEQUAL ANGLES
30°   45°

PLAN OBLIQUE
PLAN IS ROTATED TO AN ANGLE THEN CORNERS & TOP CONSTRUCTED - ALLOWS FOR QUICK STUDY OF BUILDING SHAPE

TYPICALLY 60°   TYPICALLY 30°

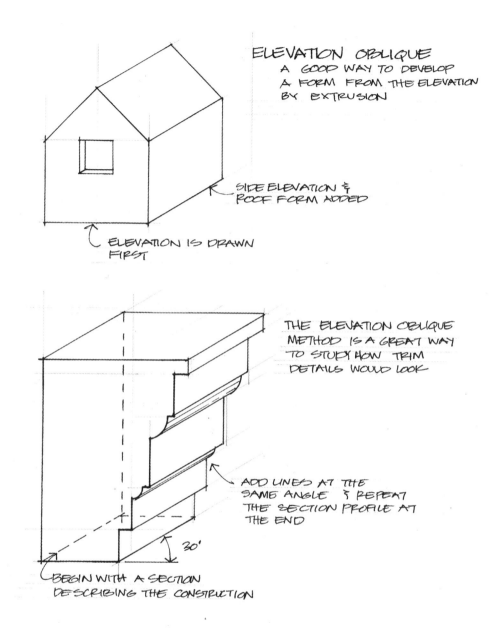

ELEVATION OBLIQUE
A GOOD WAY TO DEVELOP
A FORM FROM THE ELEVATION
BY EXTRUSION

SIDE ELEVATION &
ROOF FORM ADDED

ELEVATION IS DRAWN
FIRST

THE ELEVATION OBLIQUE
METHOD IS A GREAT WAY
TO STUDY HOW TRIM
DETAILS WOULD LOOK

ADD LINES AT THE
SAME ANGLE & REPEAT
THE SECTION PROFILE AT
THE END

30°

BEGIN WITH A SECTION
DESCRIBING THE CONSTRUCTION

Axonometric Drawing is a broad term for a paraline, non-perspective, type of drawing. The most common type used in architecture is **Isometric**, because each angle is equally foreshortened (or not at all for scaled drawings). The other two types are **Diametric** and **Trimetric**. The latter two are foreshortened in more than one axis which makes it visually distorted to the viewer.

One more comment about paraline drawings before moving on is that they do not appear to get smaller as an object moves further back into the picture, as would be the case in a perspective drawing. Rather, the object remains the same size, creating an obvious (but acceptable, in this case) distortion in reality.

Creating a Plan Oblique Drawing

Here you will take a look at the steps involved in creating a *Plan Oblique* drawing; the *Elevation Oblique* drawing is done in virtually the same way. As shown below, it is best to have the 2D views worked out before starting – at least the ones you want to see in the 3D drawing.

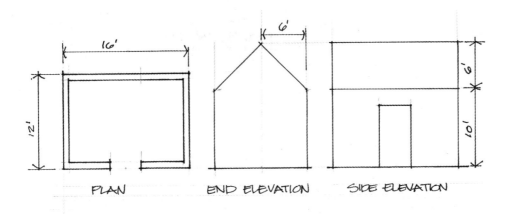

PLAN   END ELEVATION   SIDE ELEVATION

The next step involves laying out the base for your *Plan Oblique* drawing; which is a rotated version of your plan – 30 degrees off the horizontal. This is quickly drawn using a 30/60/90 triangle or tracing the rotated plan.

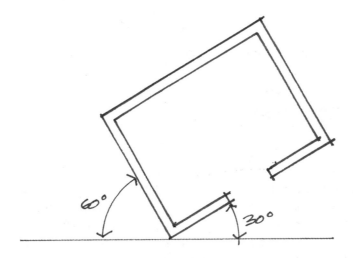

Next you draw vertical lines to represent the walls of the building. These are drawn to scale using an *Architectural Scale*. Then the "dots" are connected to form the tops of the walls as shown on the next page

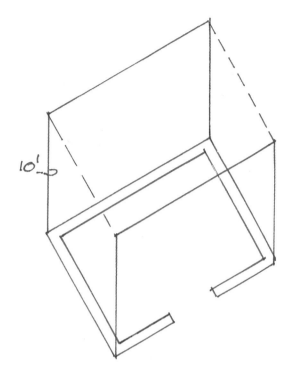

Projecting a vertical line up from the center of the gable wall you and find the peak – again using an *Architectural Scale* to accurately draw the height. Now you can connect the "dots" once again to form the gable ends of the roof and then the ridge line.

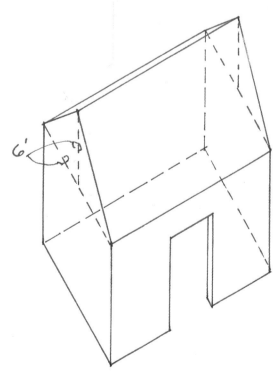

Computer Generated Isometric Drawings

Various Computer Aided Design (CAD) programs have the ability to create isometric drawings. So, in certain cases is may be easier to create the framework of your design in CAD, and then freehand sketch over a printout onto tracing paper. This would be done once you have a good idea of what you are drawing – maybe you have already generated several hand drawn options. This hybrid technique of sketching over computer drawings is covered more in chapter 13.

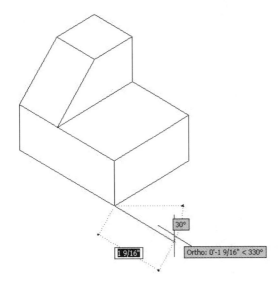

The isometric image to the left (top) was created in AutoCAD – a leading 2D/3D CAD program. This particular drawing was created using 2D tools which constrain your lines to the proper angles when in Isometric drawing mode. The obvious limitation here is that you can only view the object from this one angle (because it is 2D, not 3D) – however it is much quicker to draw than 3D.

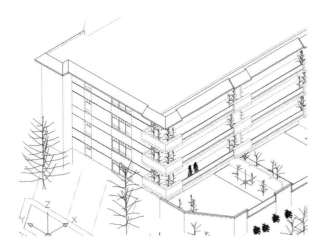

The image to the left (bottom) was also drawn in AutoCAD, but in 3D, meaning it is possible to view and print the building from multiple angles – even perspective views. A 3D drawing like this would likely take 3 times longer to draw than its 2D equivalent.

On the next page you will see a nice set of student presentation drawings exemplifying some of the techniques covered in this chapter. Take a moment and analyze the two drawings; try to figure out what part of the floor plan has been drawn in the axonometric view. Another paraline example of this project was presented in Chapter 1; flip back and find it so you can compare it to the floor plan as well.

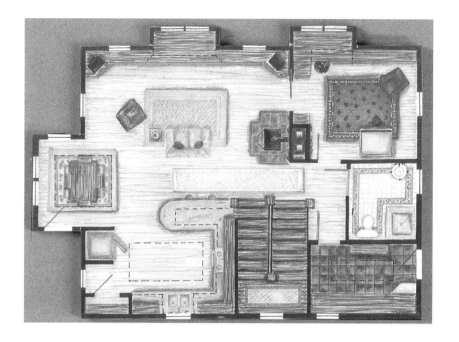

Floor plan and Axonometric drawings by **Anne Porter** CID

Adding Shadows

Architectural drawings will have a more dramatic effect on the viewer when shade and shadows are added. Sometimes shade and shadow will be superficially added just for effect; meaning it is not an accurate representation of any specific locality, month, or time of day on earth. Rather the designer is taking "artistic liberties" to make the sketch easier to understand. However, with the growing desire to conserve energy consumption, the *skilled designer* (a "skilled" designer being someone who will consider aspects of the design to create an aesthetically pleasing, efficient and functional building which will last many years) will take into account the building's orientation on the site so as to take advantage of any *Passive Solar Design* opportunities.

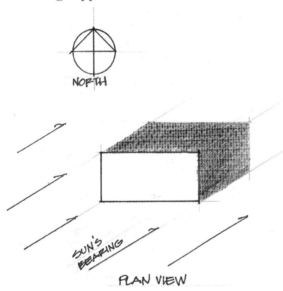

NORTH

SUN'S BEARING

PLAN VIEW

Passive Solar Design involves designing a building that will take advantage of the sun's energy without the aid of powered or mechanized equipment. For example: letting the sun's warmth in during the winter months but blocking it in the hot summer months with a sun screen. Massive stone or concrete surfaces can absorb warmth during the day and radiate that heat long into the cool night. These things and more can be employed in a building project which results in reduced energy consumption and annual financial savings for the owner – a win-win situation. These principles are not new, as the architect **Vitruvius** writes about these types of techniques in his *"Ten books on Architecture"* nearly 2000 years ago – it is just that furnaces and air conditioning made it easy to ignore those basic principles.

The drawing above shows a simple block. Without shadows, the viewer would not have any idea that the shape had any depth (or height). However, with the shadows added, it is easy to see that the block has volume.

It is not readily ascertainable as to how tall the object is because the date and time are not provided; the shadow would be shorter when the sun is higher in the sky and longer in the morning and afternoon when the sun is lower.

It is always good to provide a north arrow in plan views to keep yourself and others properly orientated.

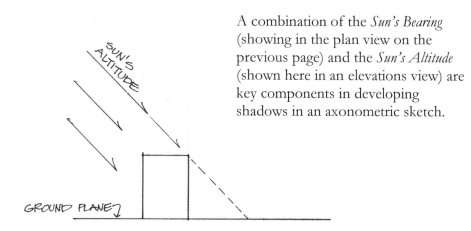

SUN'S ALTITUDE

GROUND PLANE

ELEVATION VIEW

A combination of the *Sun's Bearing* (showing in the plan view on the previous page) and the *Sun's Altitude* (shown here in an elevations view) are key components in developing shadows in an axonometric sketch.

The intersection of the *Sun's Bearing* and the *Sun's Altitude* determines the extents of the shadow. Additionally, as you can see here, lines matching the altitude and bearing angles are projected off the building's outermost points using a straightedge.

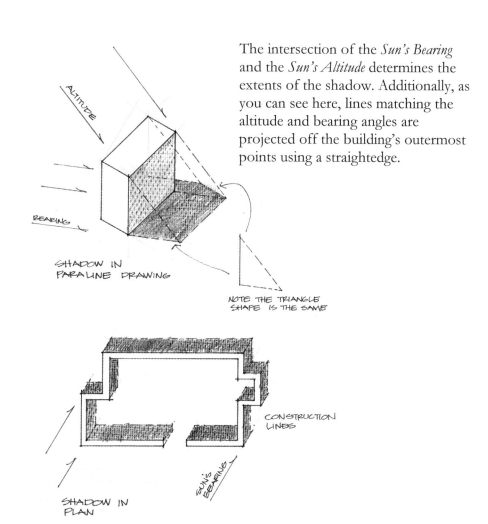

ALTITUDE

BEARING

SHADOW IN PARALINE DRAWING

NOTE THE TRIANGLE SHAPE IS THE SAME

CONSTRUCTION LINES

SHADOW IN PLAN

SUN'S BEARING

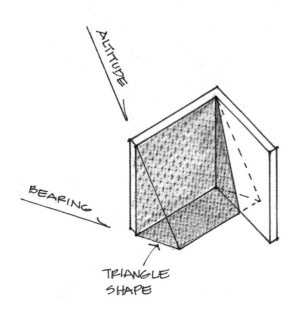

Here is an example of a shadow being projected onto an adjacent surface. The dashed lines show the extents of the shadow if the adjacent surface (i.e., the other wall) was not there. Notice how you simply "connect the dots".

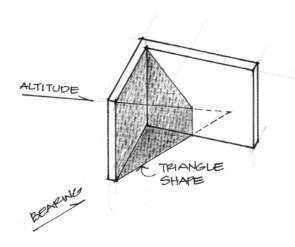

The pictures presented here generally speak for themselves. Notice in this example the adjacent wall has a different shaped shadow due to the altitude and bearing angles. The previous example could have the same shadow-shape if the sun were lower and the bearing rotated slightly. Again, the dashed lines represent the shadow extents if the adjacent wall was omitted.

Shade vs. Shadow… the surfaces opposite the light source (i.e., the sun) is in *Shade* whereas the darker areas created on the ground and various surfaces by the absence of light (i.e., the sun being blocked by something) is in *Shadow*. This is illustrated in the photo on the next page; note that the photo is a perspective view (rather than a paraline view). Shadows in perspective views are created in a fashion similar to paraline drawings. Learning the basics at shadow casting in paraline drawing will prepare you for shadows in perspective. Shadows in perspective are subject to foreshortening as they go away from you, just as other objects are. The lines defining shadows simply converge at a Vanishing Point in perspective drawing, unlike paraline drawings.

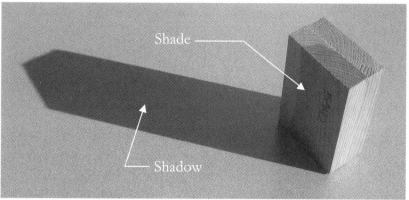

Shade vs. Shadow Example

Notice how the lines defining the edge of the shadow are tending to converge.

The two sketches here show the same object, each with a different sun condition. Focus on how the shadows are derived from projecting the *Altitude* and *Bearing* rays, creation of a specific triangle shape, and then "connecting the dots". You will get a chance to try these techniques in the chapter end exercises.

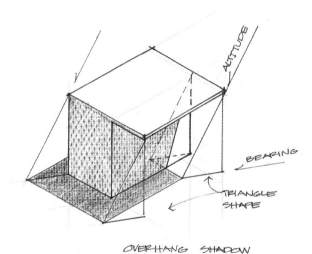

OVERHANG SHADOW

This next example (bottom right) has the sun lower in the sky than the previous example. This could be due to the time of day or season. The sun is lower in the sky in the morning and evening (time of day) and it is also lower in the sky in the winter vs. the summer – at noon (season). These examples give you an idea of how a sun screen over a window could block the hot summer sun but also let the warm sun's rays in during the winter.

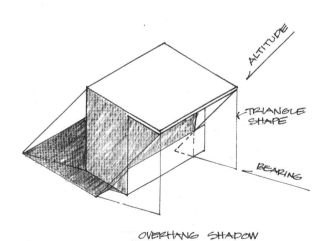

OVERHANG SHADOW

This last example on developing shadows is really just more of the same. The one thing to look at here is the deeper shadow as a result of the sun's rays having to travel further before hitting the surface. Everything is still based on projecting the altitude and bearing lines, defining the specific triangle this creates, and then "connecting the dots". Notice how the shadow line is at an angle on the vertical part of the stairs (i.e., the riser) which relates to the varying depth of the surface.

In an actual sketch you would draw the reference/construction lines much lighter so they are barely visible; they are shown darker here so the reader can clearly see them.

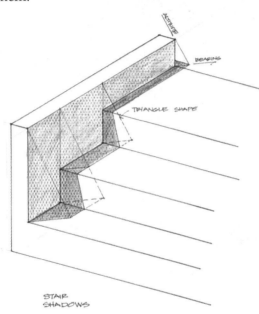

The easiest way to draft the reference/construction lines used to develop shadows is to use plastic triangles and a T-Square (see Chapter 1).

It is useful to know the fundamentals of shadows for quick sketches. However, more refined sketches are often started based on a CAD type underlay for the major elements. This gives you the proper perspective and shadows to sketch over and embellish upon. As mentioned previously in this chapter, you will learn more about this "Computer Underlay Method" in Chapter 13.

Shadows in perspective

Below are two images showing the fundamentals of shadows in perspective. This will make more sense after learning about creating perspectives later in the text.

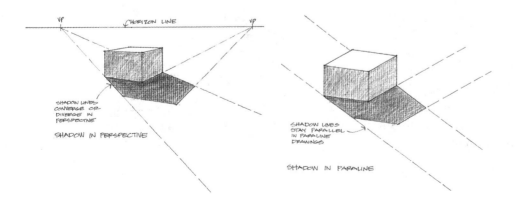

NAME_____ DATE_____

Exercise 7-1

Shadows

Add shadows to the two objects below. Use a different *altitude* and *bearing* angle for each example. Assume that the sun is generally coming over your left shoulder.

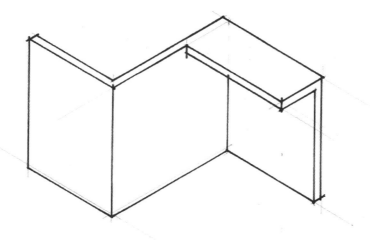

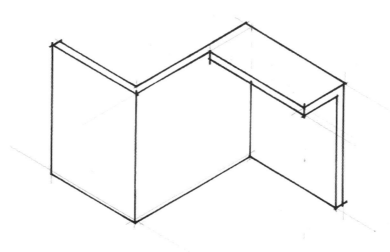

Chapter 7 **EXERCISES**

~blank page~

NAME_____ DATE_____

Exercise 7-2

Shadows

Add shadows to the exterior elevation below. Note that some of the building's surfaces may be projecting and some windows may be recessed (you decide). Assume that the sun is generally coming over your left shoulder.

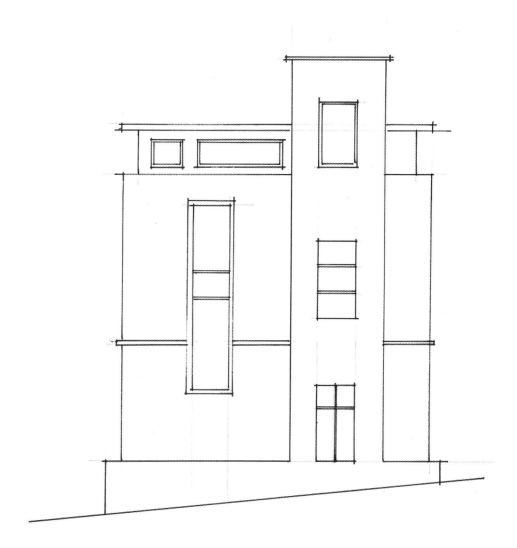

~blank page~

NAME_____ DATE_____

Exercise 7-3

Shadows
REVERSED EXAMPLE – whatever was projected in the previous example is now recessed, and visa versa.

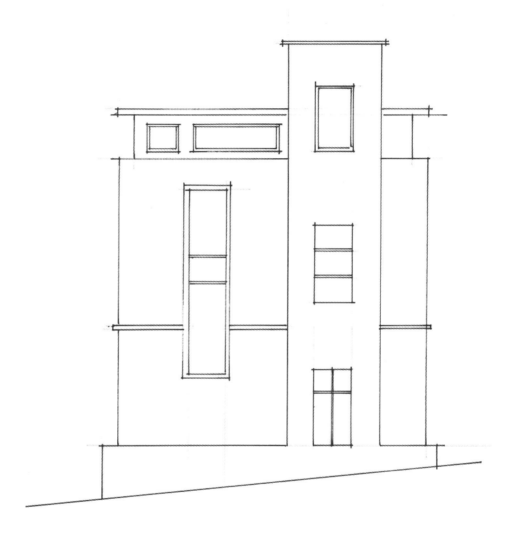

~blank page~

NAME_____ DATE_____

Exercise 7-4

Elevation Oblique Drawing
Use the information in the sketch below to create an *Elevation Oblique* drawing.

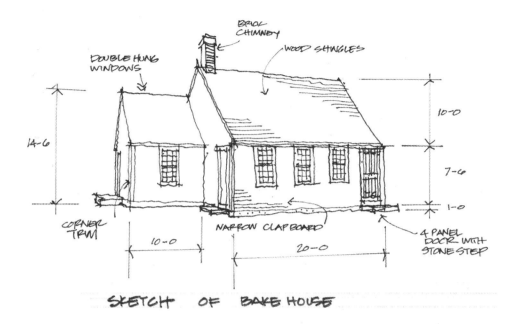

~blank page~

NAME_____ DATE_____

Exercise 7-5

Isometric Drawing

Take this quick sketch and turn it into an isometric drawing using the 30 degree grid shown. Do not worry about scale, but rather capture the basic elements including the windows.

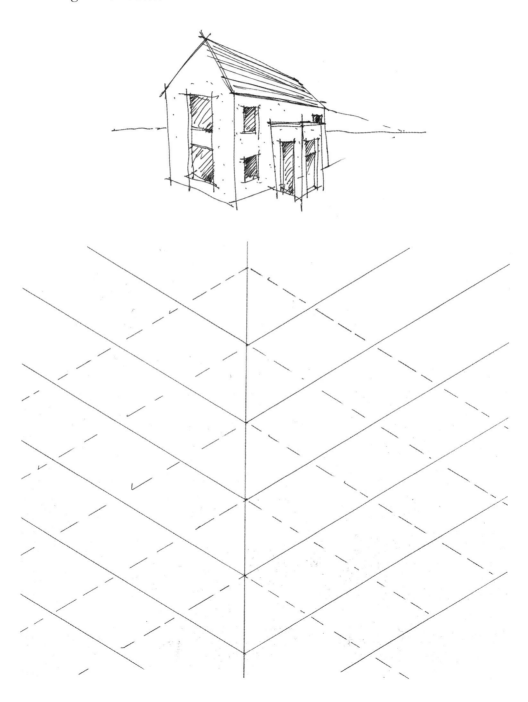

~blank page~

NAME_____ DATE_____

Self-Exam:
The following questions can be used as a way to check your knowledge of this lesson. The answers can be found at the lower left this page.

1. Shade and Shadow are the same thing. (T/F)

2. Objects appear to get smaller as they move back into the picture in a paraline (or isometric) drawing. (T/F)

3. Isometric drawings are mainly created using straightedges. (T/F)

4. An _____ drawing can be created using only a 30° triangle.

5. Surfaces opposite the light source are in _____.

Review Questions:
The following questions may be assigned by your instructor as a way to assess your knowledge of this section. Your instructor has the answers to the review questions.

1. Shadows are created by objects blocking light. (T/F)

2. An *Architectural Scale* is used when creating a *Plan Oblique* drawing. (T/F)

3. The most life-like drawing is an Isometric drawing. (T/F)

4. Several CAD programs have a special "ISO" mode to aid in the creation of isometric drawings. (T/F)

5. It is a waste of time to worry about *Passive Solar Design*. (T/F)

6. It helps to know which direction is north when delineating shadows. (T/F)

7. An *Oblique Elevation* begins with a section describing the construction. (T/F)

8. This text does not recommend using a computer to create isometric drawings. (T/F)

9. It is best to have the 2D views worked out before starting a Plan Oblique drawing. (T/F)

10. Name the three types of Axonometric drawing types mentioned:

    _____, _____, _____

~blank page~

Chapter

8

The Perspective: Two-Point I

*At this point you should have a comfort level with your pen
sufficient to begin exploring the fundamentals of the perspective
drawing. This is an exciting step in learning to draw because you
can see the drawings begin to "come to life"!*

A perspetive drawing is a two-dimensional drawing which represents a
three-dimensional object or scene *and* takes into account the phenomenon
that things appear to get smaller the further they are from the viewer.
There's a bit more to it than that (which you will cover in this chapter), but this is
a working definition we will start with. Additionally, a perspective drawing looks
very much like what we perceive when looking at the world.

Below are the three primary types of perspective created by Architectural
Designers: *[from left to right]* one-point, two-point and three-point perspectives.

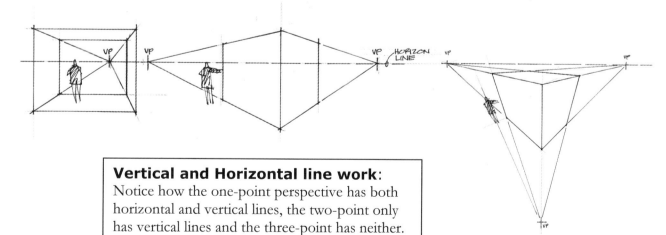

Vertical and Horizontal line work:
Notice how the one-point perspective has both
horizontal and vertical lines, the two-point only
has vertical lines and the three-point has neither.

The Horizon Line

One of the first things you need to understand when it comes to perspective drawing is the *Horizon Line* – what it is and how it relates to the drawing. In the simplest of terms, the *Horizon Line* is the edge of the earth; at least the edge as it is perceived from the eye. As the earth curves away from any one person's view, they see a distinct line between the earth and the sky. Even though the earth is round, it is so large that it appears to be flat. When drawing a perspective drawing this important reference line is assumed to be flat (i.e., horizontal).

In most perspectives, renderings and photographs you don't usually see the *Horizon Line* because it is obscured by trees, hills, buildings, etc. However, there are some cases in which you do see it, such as when you have the ocean or a vast field as a backdrop to your building.

The photo below helps to understand the *Horizon Line* by providing a real-world example. This example is of a building pictured with a large body of water behind it (this is not an ocean, but it is the largest freshwater lake in the world – by surface area – Lake Superior). Notice the *Horizon Line* labeled in the picture.

Horizon
Line

Understanding the Horizon Line

Another quick example of the *Horizon Line* is shown in the photo below. A simple picnic bench is not much different than a building when it comes to perspective; it has four sides and a top.

You should pay close attention to the sketched overlays on this page and the previous one. These overlays should make clear the close relationship between a hand drawn perspective (which you will learn how to do in this chapter) and a photograph (or, better, what you see with your eyes)!

Understanding the Horizon Line

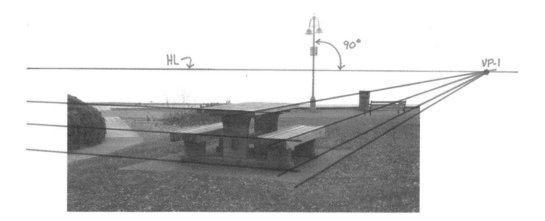

The **Vanishing Point** is not something visible as is the *Horizon Line*. However it is possible to locate the *Vanishing Points* by extending lines back until they converge (as shown above). The lines will always converge on the *Horizon Line* and thus reveal the *Vanishing Point* for the object under consideration.

The Two-Point Perspective

Two-point perspective drawings are two-dimensional drawings that represent three-dimensional objects or scenes. As the name implies, there are two points, referred to as *Vanishing Points* – VP. These points establish the perspective lines which are both relative to a *Horizon Line* (HL). The object being depicted has three primary types of lines:

- *Perspective lines,* which always converge at the *Vanishing Points.*
- *Vertical lines,* which are always truly vertical to the page.
- *Angled lines,* which are usually drawn by 'connecting-the-dots' via line work fully developed from the previous two line types.

Two-point perspective drawings are primarily meant for rectilinear objects. For example, a uniform series of blocks can be sketched much easier than an 'organic' shaped suburban development.

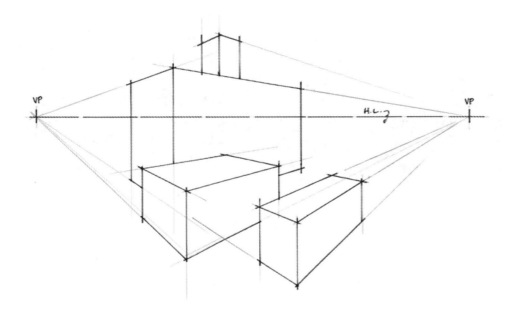

The concepts covered can be applied to more detailed embellishments such as windows and siding, sidewalks and driveways, fences and garages.

In the image above you should take a moment to notice a few things:
1) All lines are either vanishing or perfectly vertical.
2) Anything drawn outside of an imaginary circle (actually shown on the next page) is too distorted and should be avoided.
3) Objects completely below the horizon are as viewed from the top (aerial view, like from an airplane), and objects completely above are as viewed from below (worm's eye view). You can quickly create rectilinear objects in any shape or size by sketching the vanishing lines and vertical lines as shown!

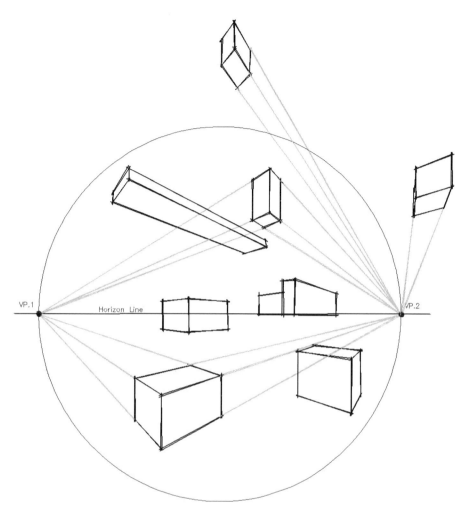

Two-Point Perspective

The following exercise will walk you through the steps required to develop a two-point perspective of the exterior of a residence. You are encouraged to following

along on a separate piece of paper or in a sketch book. The exact dimensions and proportions do not really matter at this time as you are focusing on the mechanics of perspective drawings. Try drawing this freehand first and then try again using a straightedge.

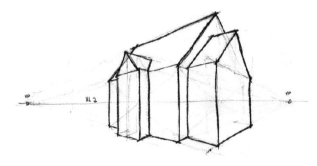

The bulleted steps on the next page relate to the 'lettered' and then 'numbered' sketches on the opposite page:

Main building with gable roof – Image A

This first step is simply sketching a basic box with a gable roof element dropped on top. You should try to make your sketch as similar as possible in terms of proportions – the vertical centerline (centered between the two *Vanishing Points*) has been added to aid in this.

1. Draw a vertical line just to the right of the 'centerline' with equal portions above and below the *Horizon Line* (see one vertical line marked with a #1).
2. Connect-the-dots: draw four lines from the *VP's* to the top and bottom of the vertical line as shown (see four lines marked with a #2).
3. Draw two vertical lines to define the overall size of the main building.
4. Draw an 'X' and a vertical line at its intersection to discern the midpoint of the gable end of the building. (**Note**: It is not the midpoint of the bottom edge of the building – confirm this with a scale).
5. Draw the ridge line of the roof: a line from VP-1 to the vertical line sketched in the previous step. (The location of this line determines the pitch of the roof; higher = steeper.)
6. Connect-the-dots: draw lines to create the gable roof edges.
7. Lightly sketch the hidden portions of the building as shown.

Bisecting the building – Image B

Here you will learn how to find the exact middle of the building, this will help in locating the cross-gable in the next image/task.

1. Sketch an 'X' on the bottom plane of the building.
2. Draw a perspective line from VP.2 which passes through the 'X'.
3. Sketch three vertical lines as shown (the vanishing line just drawn helped establish the starting point on the front and back face of the building).
4. Connect-the-dots: from the intersection of the roof and three vertical lines.

FYI: The two visible bisecting lines have an arrow at the top and bottom in this image and the next one to make them stand out – these lines will eventually be erased.

Adding cross-gable entry – Image C

Next you will sketch in the "bump out" on the front of the building.

1. This perspective line (*from VP.1*) determines how far "out" the "bump" will be.
2. Draw two vertical lines a certain distance apart and approximately centered on the main building (you will learn to be more precise later).
3. Draw two perspective lines (*from VP.2*) to establish the bottom edges.
4. Draw a vertical line up to the roof edge – from the intersection of the perspective line just drawn and the bottom front edge of the main building.
5. Do the same as step three to establish the top edges (*from VP.2*)
6. Draw this perspective line (*from VP.1*) to verify the top-front edge is correct.
7. Use the 'X' method to discern the center of the gable wall.
8. Sketch the ridge line of the entry roof – the location determines roof slope.
9. Connect-the-dots: the remaining valley lines can be easily drawn.

All lines should be sketched very lightly with pencil and the visible lines can be made darker at the end, as well as erasing the unneeded reference lines and hidden lines.

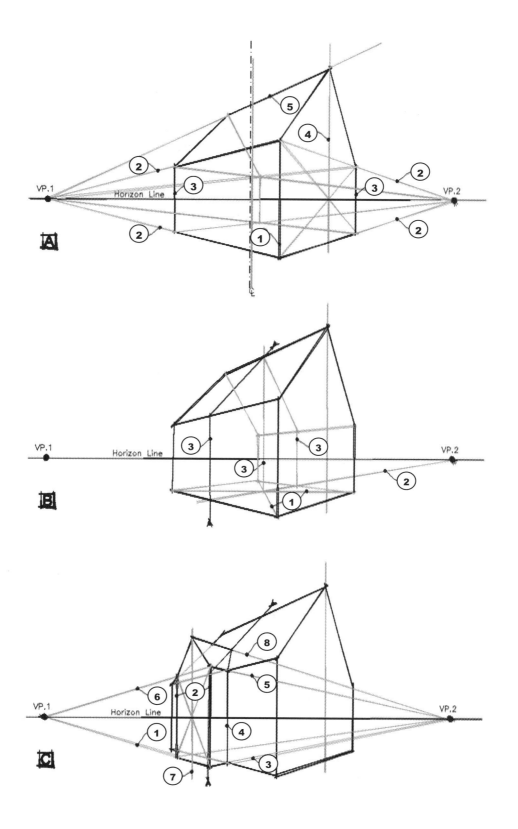

Centered and symmetrical addition – Image D

The following steps show you how to make an extrusion off the main building which is symmetrical. You cannot measure in from each side an equal distance because things get closer together as you approach the *Vanishing Points*.

1. The first line (*from VP.2*) will determine how large the extrusion (or addition) will be from the main mass of the residence.
2. Here you will basically extend the front and back bottom (i.e., grade) line out to the previous line drawn. (Sketch lightly as these lines will be erased.)
3. Draw an 'X' in the large, flat, rectangle just created.
4. Now you will draw a vanishing line (*from VP.2*) near the building. The intersection of this line and the 'X' lines will establish the front and back wall locations for the addition (which will be drawn in the next step).
5. Draw two lines (*from VP.1*) so that they pass through the intersection of the 'X' (from step 3) and the perspective line (from step 4), and terminate these lines at the perspective line drawn in step 1) – as shown in image D.

Completing the massing of the addition – Image E

Now that the footprint of the addition is sufficiently developed you can create the remaining line work.

1. Draw four vertical lines as shown.
2. Draw a perspective line (if needed – i.e., if you erased the previous one you drew) – from VP.2 to the roof edge of the main building. This assumes the roof edge of the addition will align with the main building and not be lower (simply swinging this perspective line down a bit would allow for this change).
3. Draw two vanishing lines (*from VP.1*) through the line drawn in the previous step and the vertical lines at the main building (drawn in step 1).
4. Finding the middle of the gable end of the main building, you can sketch the roof slope lines. This is done in conjunction with the next step which locates the ridge line.
5. Draw the ridge line (*from VP.1*).
6. Find the middle of the gable end of the addition and finish sketching the sloped roof edges.

At this point you have developed the main masses of your structure. Now you can erase the reference lines and hidden lines, and then darken the remaining lines. Another option is to use tracing paper and a soft pencil to sketch a new image based on the 'visible' lines of your original sketch.

Again, you may use these techniques to add windows, siding, trim, chimneys and such. Here is another good use for tracing paper: you can sketch different window and siding options on the tracing paper, so you don't need to start from scratch with the base model every time!

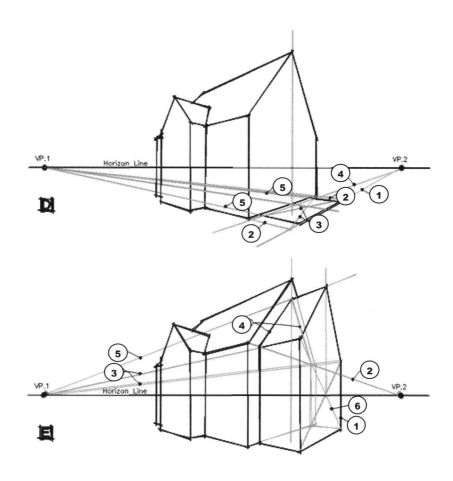

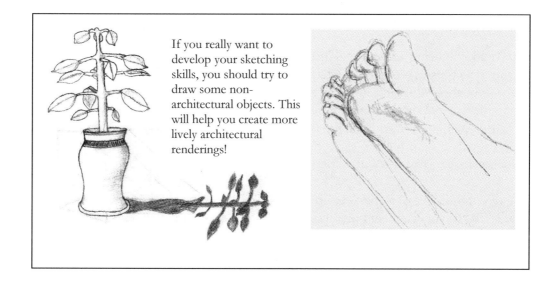

If you really want to develop your sketching skills, you should try to draw some non-architectural objects. This will help you create more lively architectural renderings!

The Human Scale Method

One challenge we often have when sketching in perspective is making all the various parts at the proper scale. This gets easier with practice and experience, but until then you need to be able to use a few tricks to establish scale or even to double check parts of your previously drawn perspective. In this section you will learn about a technique called the **Human Scale Method**, which uses a 6 foot tall measuring stick (i.e., a person) to size up objects in the perspective.

When sketching a building, a designer may get the overall building correct, but then they may make the windows too small or the door too large; this has a negative impact on the perceived aesthetics of the design. The *Human Scale Method* projects the height of a person around the scene to compare and verify vertical heights. For example, if you project the six foot person's height onto the face of your building and the second floor windows are not approximately "another person" in height above (i.e., 12 feet total) something is probably wrong.

In the following tutorial you will learn how to create a simple rectangular building with a gable roof using the *Human Scale Method*.

Step A – the horizon, a vanishing point, and a person

Before you begin drawing, you should remember you are not creating presentation drawings, so remember to work fast, keep it loose and don't get bogged down! The example drawings in this section have been drawn with a straight edge just to make things very clear to you, but it is still all hand drawn.

Start out by drawing a horizontal line; this is the *horizon*. Next, you will sketch a gesture type person (covered in Chapter 2) with the head on the horizon (you will learn more about this later in the *Entourage* section). The size of the person will dictate the overall size of the sketch so try to make it just the right size, which will allow the building to mostly fill the page - not so large it will not fit on the paper or too small that it is hard to show the proper level of detail; the only "right" answer is that this comes with experience.

The next fundamental step to set up your perspective is to locate the *Vanishing Points* (VP) so you can begin projecting lines. Where do you put the *Vanishing Points*? If you are close to the object, the *Vanishing Points* are further apart, and if you are further away the VP's are closer together.

The example directly below shows one *Vanishing Point* on the left, the *Horizon Line* and a person who we will assume is 6'-0" tall. The other *Vanishing Point* will be added later.

Just so you know, even though the horizon actually curves with the surface of the earth, we always draw a horizontal line as the curve is not perceived by the eye. Also, this view would be from another person's perspective – which is why the head is on the horizon. If the view was from an airplane, the head would be well below the *Horizon Line* (if the HL showed up at all).

Step B – project the person back to one vanishing point

Now that you have the *Horizon Line*, a *Vanishing Point* and a person sketched, you can project a set of lines from the feet and head of your person back to one of the *Vanishing Points*. Obviously the person's feet are on the ground, so the line from the feet to the *Vanishing Point* is also on the ground. From this "grounded" line you can project lines up to start your building. In this example the head is on the *Horizon Line* so you do not really need to project any lines from the head.

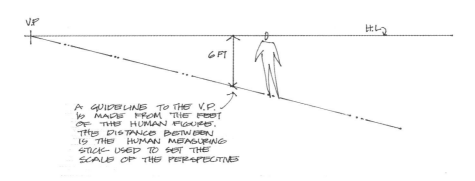

Step C – determine the required height

Using the approximate size of your human measuring stick, you can easily sketch additional vanishing lines to establish various heights. Remember, the height stays constant along a vertical line; notice the various 6'-0" tall lines in the image below. For example, imagine the gesture person below with another person standing on his shoulders. This second person's head would (or should) align with the next vanishing line above.

In the next section, after the *Human Scale Method*, you will study how to divide faces and spaces into smaller segments; which will allow more accuracy in your sketch.

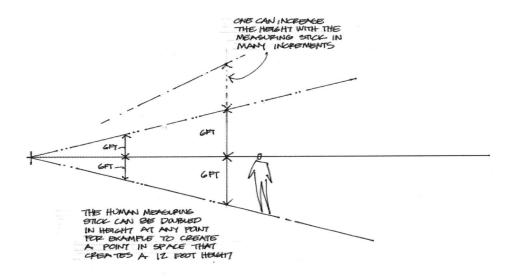

Step D – describing a surface

Now you can draw vertical lines, using the *Vanishing Lines* for reference. Once these vertical lines hit the other *Vanishing Line* (i.e., off the persons head, which is on the HL), you have made a six foot tall line. On one vertical line the scale does not change (like it does in plan) so you can use that 6 foot measure to establish the height of the building (e.g., 2 units = 12' or 3 units = 18').

As you can see in the image on the next page, a surface is described by drawing two vertical lines and then "connecting the dots" along the vanishing lines.

In a similar fashion, you can establish another *Vanishing Point* and develop the adjacent surface.

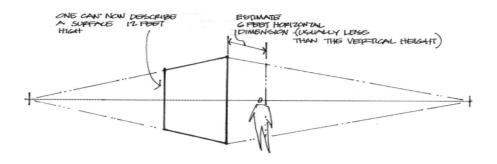

Step E – additional six foot squares

Using the method shown graphically below, you can add additional 6′ x 6′ surfaces (additional information is provided on Dividing Spaces in the next section). Notice this works in perspective as well as in flat two dimensional drawings (the sketch in the lower left is such a flat drawing).

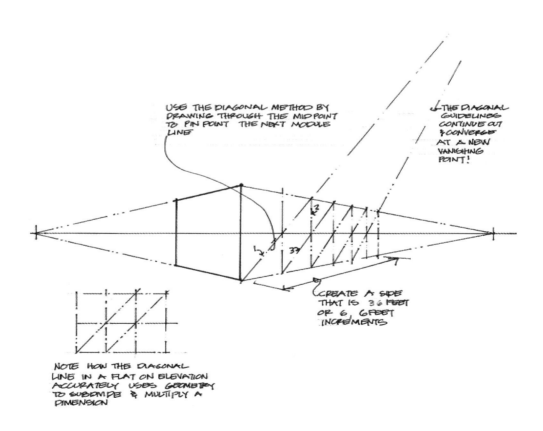

Step F – gable roof edge

Once you have your primary box established you are now in a position to develop the gable roof edge. As shown (and numbered) below, you can draw an "X" on the surface from corner to corner. Now draw a vertical line which passes through the intersection of the two diagonal lines. Finally you draw the diagonal lines that form the edge of the gable roof.

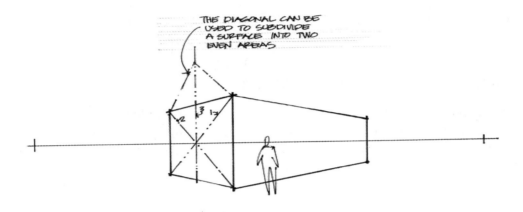

THE DIAGONAL CAN BE USED TO SUBDIVIDE A SURFACE INTO TWO EVEN AREAS

Step G – dividing a surface into odd numbers

If you already have the overall surface described and you want to add an odd number of vertical lines, then do this:

1. Divide the vertical line into the number of spaces desired. As you should recall, the length is consistent along the length of the vertical lines in a two-point perspective. Therefore you can use a scale if you want to be very accurate or you may eyeball it seeing as things are not distorted. In any case, make a small tick on the vertical lines for reference.

2. Draw lines from the tick marks, made in the previous step, back to the *Vanishing Point*. In the image on the top of the next page there are two ticks, with two corresponding lines extending to the *Vanishing Point*. These lines should be very light on your drawing as they are only for reference.

3. Draw a diagonal line across the surface under consideration. This should also be a rather light line which is only for reference.

4. Sketch vertical lines wherever a vanishing line (drawn in step 2) intersects the diagonal line (drawn in step 3).

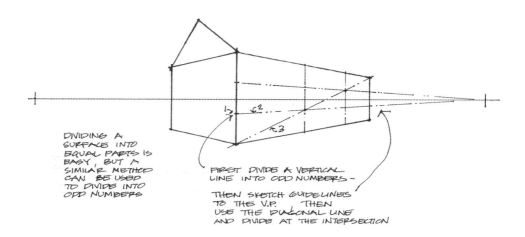

DIVIDING A SURFACE INTO EQUAL PARTS IS EASY, BUT A SIMILAR METHOD CAN BE USED TO DIVIDE INTO ODD NUMBERS

FIRST DIVIDE A VERTICAL LINE INTO ODD NUMBERS –

THEN SKETCH GUIDELINES TO THE V.P. THEN USE THE DIAGONAL LINE AND DIVIDE AT THE INTERSECTION

Step H – completing the gable roof

Finishing the roof consists, mostly, of connecting the dots. First you sketch a line from the peak of the gable roof (drawn in step F) back to the *Vanishing Point*. The last edge to be defined (the back edge in this example – below) is almost parallel to the front edge; this line is usually approximated.

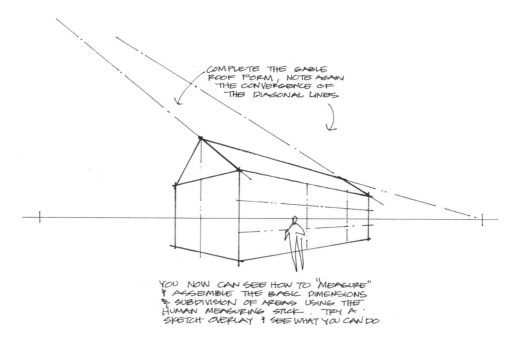

COMPLETE THE GABLE ROOF FORM, NOTE AGAIN THE CONVERGENCE OF THE DIAGONAL LINES

YOU NOW CAN SEE HOW TO "MEASURE" & ASSEMBLE THE BASIC DIMENSIONS & SUBDIVISION OF AREAS USING THE HUMAN MEASURING STICK. TRY A SKETCH OVERLAY & SEE WHAT YOU CAN DO

Once you have the *Human Scale* defined on one surface you can project it around the corner and onto other surfaces. To do this you simply project a line from the intersection of the previously draw lines back to the other *Vanishing Point*.

Finally, you may firm up the major lines. Use a rolling parallel rule to add vertical siding (as shown below) and roofing if the perspective is not too sharp (otherwise the lines are not parallel).

We will cover a little more on this after the next section on *Dividing Spaces*.

The end result is an accurately scaled two-point perspective drawing. You will be presented with several exercises on this method to help drive the concept home!

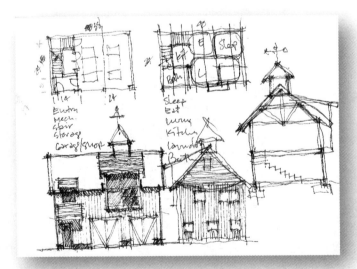

Study Sketches by ***Darryl Booker***,
Associate Professor, North Dakota State University

NAME_____ DATE_____

Exercise 8-1

Discover the Horizon Line / Create Boxes from Rectangles
The first task in this exercise is to discover the Horizon Line. This is done by projecting vanishing lines back towards the vanishing point; where the lines converge is where the vanishing point is. You will need to tear this page out and tape it onto a larger piece of paper as the Vanishing Points will not fit on this page. The second task is to turn these surfaces into three-dimensional objects – you decide the depth to show.

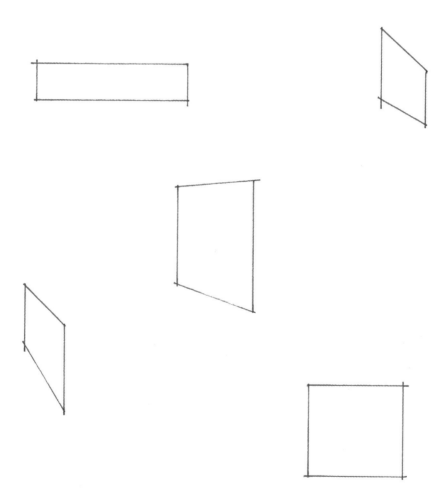

~blank page~

NAME_____ DATE_____

Exercise 8-2

Storyboard Exercise – Data
Make a few copies of this page and try sketching some rectangular shapes similar to those shown at the beginning of Chapter 8. Try to create your own variations on this theme.

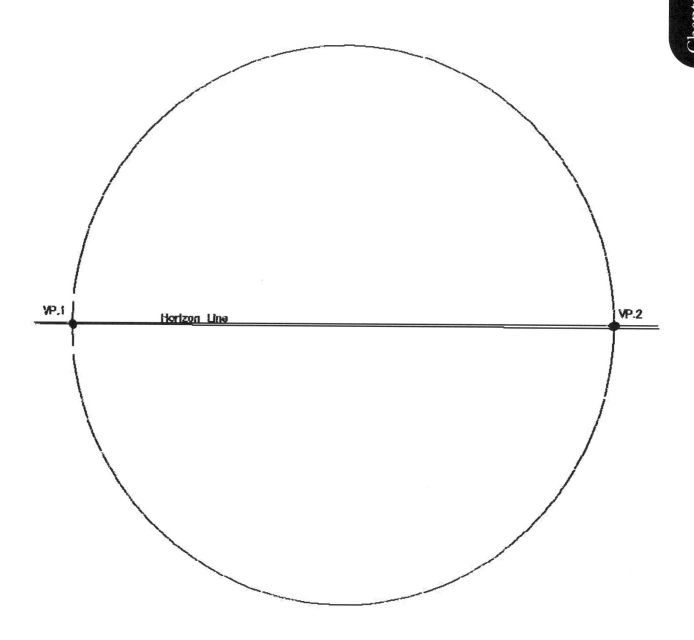

VP.1   Horizon Line   VP.2

~blank page~

NAME_____ DATE_____

Exercise 8-3

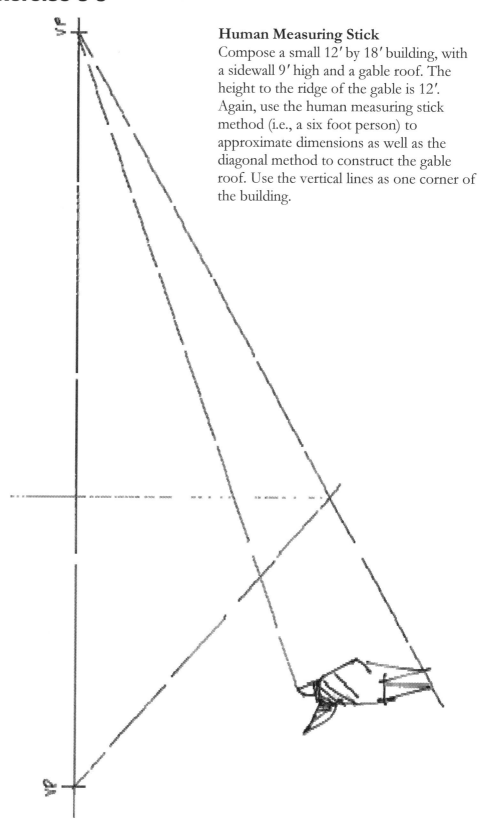

Human Measuring Stick
Compose a small 12′ by 18′ building, with a sidewall 9′ high and a gable roof. The height to the ridge of the gable is 12′. Again, use the human measuring stick method (i.e., a six foot person) to approximate dimensions as well as the diagonal method to construct the gable roof. Use the vertical lines as one corner of the building.

~blank page~

NAME_____ DATE_____

Exercise 8-4

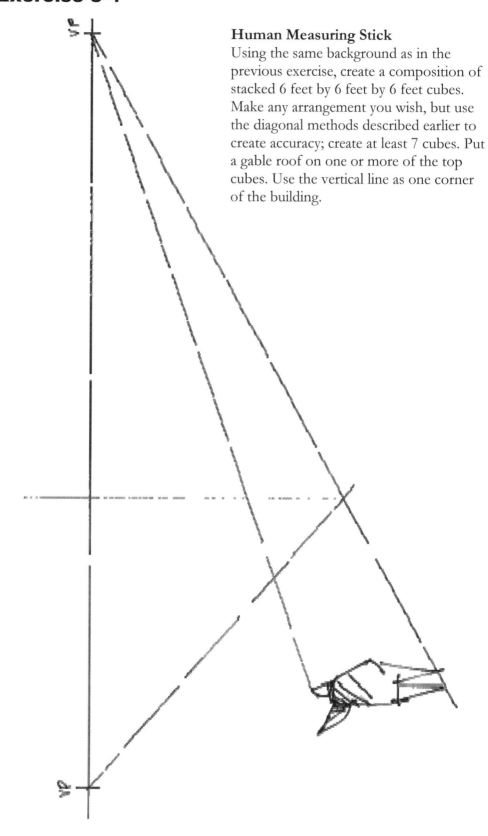

Human Measuring Stick
Using the same background as in the previous exercise, create a composition of stacked 6 feet by 6 feet by 6 feet cubes. Make any arrangement you wish, but use the diagonal methods described earlier to create accuracy; create at least 7 cubes. Put a gable roof on one or more of the top cubes. Use the vertical line as one corner of the building.

~blank page~

NAME_____ DATE_____

Exercise 8-5

Human Measuring Stick

Using the human figure as a 6 foot measuring stick, construct a two-point perspective of a block 18′ high, 12′ wide and 18′ deep with a 9′ high (and 3′ wide) door in one wall. Use the diagonal method to accurately repeat the human measuring stick modules. Use the vertical line provided as one corner.

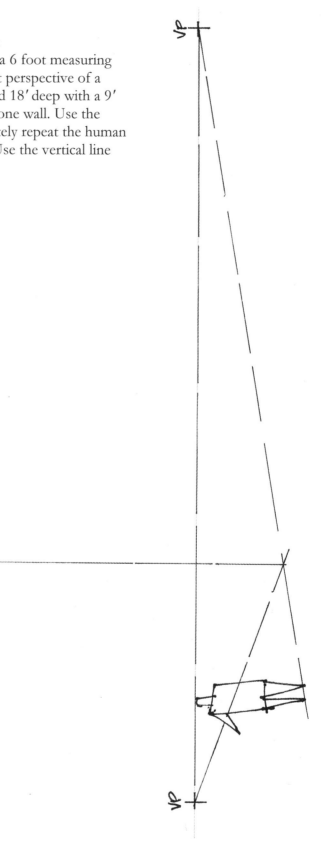

~blank page~

NAME_____ DATE_____

Self-Exam:

The following questions can be used as a way to check your knowledge of this lesson. The answers can be found at the lower left on this page.

1. It is not possible to find the *Vanishing Points* in a printed photograph. (T/F)

2. The three types of perspectives are: 1-, 2- and 3-point. (T/F)

3. It is not possible to sketch equal spaces which step back into the perspective view. (T/F)

4. In a 2-point perspective, all lines are either vanishing or _____.

5. _____-point perspectives have both horizontal and vertical lines.

Review Questions:

The following questions may be assigned by your instructor as a way to assess your knowledge of this section. Your instructor has the answers to the review questions.

1. All lines converge in 3-point perspectives. (T/F)

2. In the *Human Scale* method, the [human's] head is aligned with the *Horizon Line* for eye-level drawings. (T/F)

3. Rectangular shapes are sketched more easily than are organic shapes with the 2-point perspective method. (T/F)

4. In a photograph, one does not usually see the horizon line. (T/F)

5. In a 2-point perspective, the two vanishing points are not always on the *Horizon Line*. (T/F)

6. The main value in the _____ _____ method is making the various parts of the drawing the proper size.

7. Sketching an "X" on a surface in perspective locates the center. (T/F)

8. 3-point perspectives have vertical line work in them. (T/F)

9. It is possible to reveal the *Horizon Line* in a photograph. (T/F)

10. In a 2-point perspective, the length is consistent along any given vertical line. (T/F)

Self-Exam Answers:
1 - F, **2** - T, **3** - F, **4** - Vertical, **5** – One

Chapter 8 **Questions**

~blank page~

The Perspective: Two-Point II

Sketching should be fun; the idea of bringing your ideas to life on paper can be very rewarding – both emotionally and financially. One of the key ingredients in making sketching fun is understanding the fundamental concepts so you are not struggling or "spinning your wheels", as the saying goes.

With the advent of the computer there has been a steady shift toward the use of computers in the design process. There is nothing wrong with that. In fact, the accuracy and speed in which construction drawings can be created has given the industry a real boost. However, there is still a place for hand sketching and many designers are missing this opportunity and starting the design process on the computer. As is mentioned several times in this text, there needs to be a proper balance between hand sketching and Computer Aided Design (CAD).

Understanding several fundamental concepts and techniques (or shortcuts) is a key factor in being efficient with, and generally having fun at, hand sketching. This chapter will continue to build on the skills you learned in the previous chapter.

In this chapter we will cover the *Rapson* method. With this skill you will be better equipped to quickly transfer the ideas in your mind to understandable 2D images on paper. You will better be able to explore many more ideas than you would with a computer for the beginning of the design process. In the end, having explored more options, you should have a more elegant design solution: beautiful, weather tight, energy efficient and on budget!

Repeating spaces in perspective

The following steps will talk you through the process of repeating a shape equally as it moves towards the *Vanishing Point*. This is how you might sketch railroad tracks or a picket fence. In this example you will be applying this concept to an interior elevation of base cabinets.

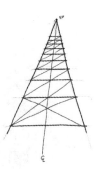

Adding additional spaces of equal size:
1. Sketch an 'X' in a rectangular space (a square in this example).
2. Add a horizontal line which passes through the center of the 'X'.
3. Draw a diagonal line from the upper left, so that it passes through the intersection of the horizontal line (from the previous step) and the right edge of the square. Continue this angle until you hit the bottom edge of the square (you need to extend the top and bottom lines as shown).
4. Sketch a new vertical line where the diagonal line meets the bottom horizontal line.
5. Repeat this process for additional segments.

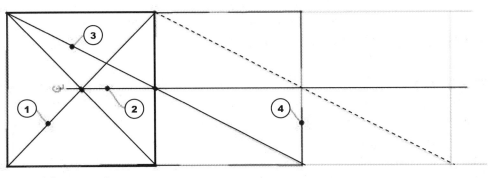

[first square]

Now you can apply this technique to surfaces that are in perspective. You can use the techniques described on the following page to finish the image which has been started for you below. **FYI:** Make a few photocopies if you think you need to try it more than once; also you can enlarge the image that way.

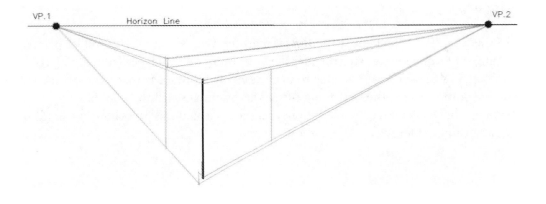

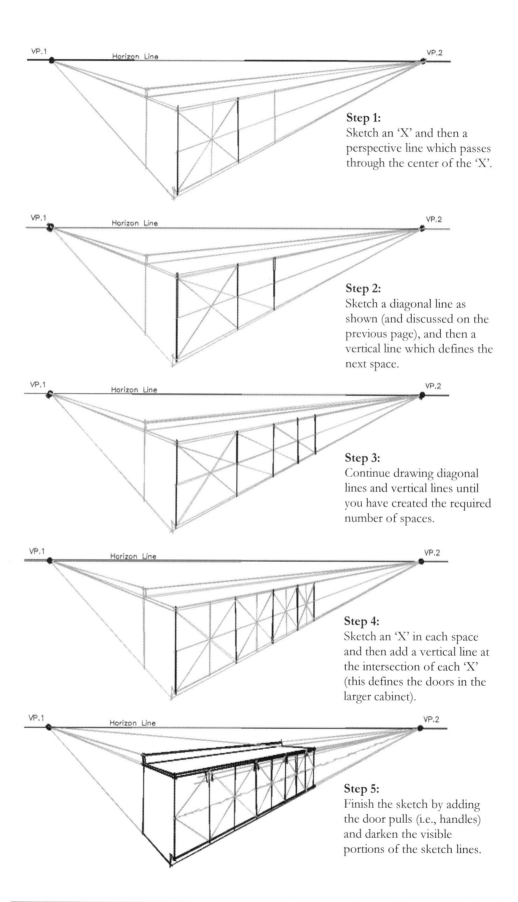

Step 1:
Sketch an 'X' and then a perspective line which passes through the center of the 'X'.

Step 2:
Sketch a diagonal line as shown (and discussed on the previous page), and then a vertical line which defines the next space.

Step 3:
Continue drawing diagonal lines and vertical lines until you have created the required number of spaces.

Step 4:
Sketch an 'X' in each space and then add a vertical line at the intersection of each 'X' (this defines the doors in the larger cabinet).

Step 5:
Finish the sketch by adding the door pulls (i.e., handles) and darken the visible portions of the sketch lines.

Casting Rays

There are several ways in which you can develop a perspective drawing; some are more complex and time consuming than others. Designers tend to gravitate towards the "most bang for the buck" method, meaning that they achieve the best looking drawings with the least amount of effort and time. The next method you will study is *Casting Rays*, which is one of those more time-consuming exercises not used all that often these days. So, you are thinking, why do I want to spend time learning this method? Well, you should spend the time and here's why: this is a detailed process that will help you better understand the "mechanics" of a perspective drawing. The next few pages will walk you through the process of creating an accurate perspective from a previously drawn set of 2D drawings (Floor Plan and Elevation Views). You will have an opportunity to test-drive this technique at the end of this chapter in the exercise section.

Casting Rays: Step 1 – 2D Plans and Elevations

The first step in using the **Casting Rays** method is to have a set of two-dimensional views which have been drawn to scale (note that they must be the same scale). You will need a floor plan and exterior elevations; you will only need to have the elevations that correspond to the sides of the building you will see in the perspective view. Compare this information with that presented in the next step to see how the perspective will show the front and east (or right) side of the building.

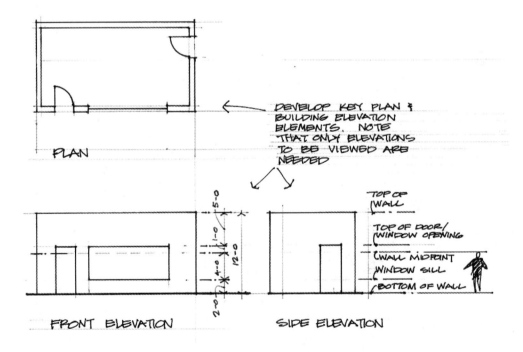

Casting Rays: Step 2 – Establish Viewpoint

Now that you have your 2D floor plans and elevations drawn you can establish the point from which to view your building. Think of it as if you have a camera in your hand and you are looking through the view finder to take a picture of the building. When you find the "perfect" picture, you have found your perspective's viewpoint.

The sketch below shows the viewpoint location. Imagine the viewpoint moving to the left; you would see the front of the building more straight-on and the side more foreshortened. The opposite is true if the viewpoint moves in the other direction.

Finally, the *Ray of View* lines are cast (i.e., sketched) from the viewpoint to the major corners of the building. These lines should be light as they are not directly used or needed in the final sketch – they are merely development lines which are used for reference.

You should plan on using a straightedge (e.g., a plastic triangle) to create these types of drawings. The last step talks about how you can use the end result as an underlay for a hand sketched final drawing.

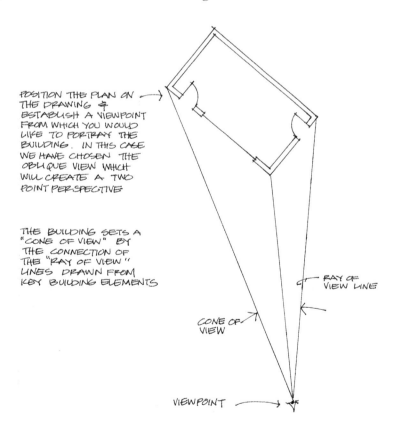

Casting Rays: Step 3 – Define the Picture Plane

This step has you establish what is called the *Picture Plane*. You can think of this plane as the surface on which the image is sketched. So the line you see (dashed) in the sketch below could be the edge of a piece of paper (i.e., a paper is tipped up on edge or perpendicular to this view).

So now imagine standing at the *Viewpoint*, looking at the building through the *Picture Plane*, and note that where the outermost *Cone of View* lines (see previous step) hit the *Picture Plane* is the extent of the image/perspective you would see on the paper.

Additionally, you need to draw two reference lines from the *Viewpoint* to the *Picture Plane*, keeping these lines parallel with the faces of the building in plan view. You will see how these are used in the next step.

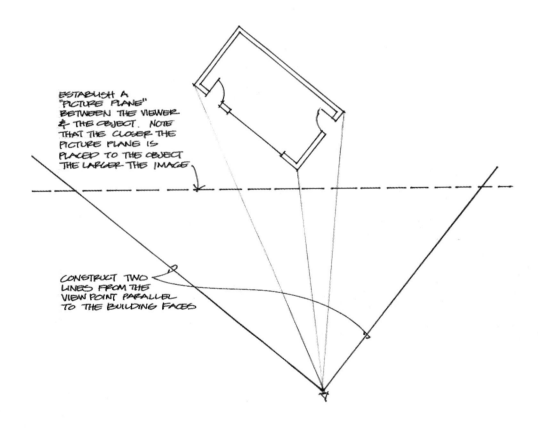

ESTABLISH A "PICTURE PLANE" BETWEEN THE VIEWER & THE OBJECT. NOTE THAT THE CLOSER THE PICTURE PLANE IS PLACED TO THE OBJECT THE LARGER THE IMAGE

CONSTRUCT TWO LINES FROM THE VIEW POINT PARALLEL TO THE BUILDING FACES

Casting Rays: Step 4 – Locate the Horizon Line and Vanishing Points

The *Horizon Line* is the next major component to be added to your perspective drawing. This horizontal line can be drawn anywhere between the *Viewpoint* and the *Picture Plane* (this is the most convenient location for it). As you should know, this line represents the edge of the Earth in the distance; this line is usually covered (whether in sketch or photo) by trees, smaller vegetation and other buildings.

In as much as you are developing a two-point perspective, you need to place two *Vanishing Points.* You will do that now. The *Vanishing Points* are located by projecting a vertical line down from the intersection of the "parallel" lines (see Step 3) and the *Picture Plane*, down to the *Horizon Line.*

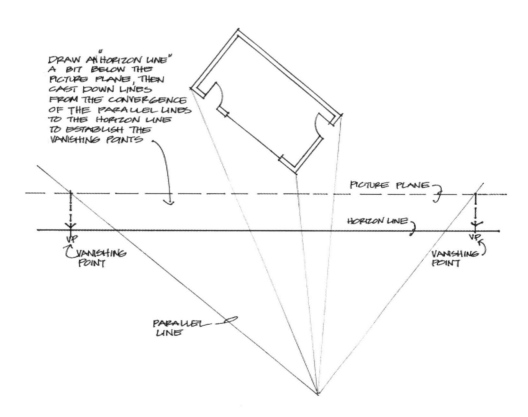

Casting Rays: Step 5 – Locate Vertical Lines

You are now ready to start placing some lines that are actually part of the building! Looking at the sketch below, you can see the task at hand is to locate the major vertical elements. This is done by projecting vertical lines down from the intersection of the various *Ray of View* lines (drawn back in Step 2) and the *Picture Plane.*

These vertical lines represent the three corners of the building. If this were a more complex building, you would just see more of the same – that is, additional *Ray of View* lines projecting from the *Viewpoint* to each corner and the vertical lines added in this step.

Again, think about all the steps you have completed thus far and you only have three vertical lines that will actually be part of the final sketch. The *Horizon Line* will technically also be part of the sketch; however, that line usually gets covered by "props" such as trees, cars, adjacent buildings, etc.

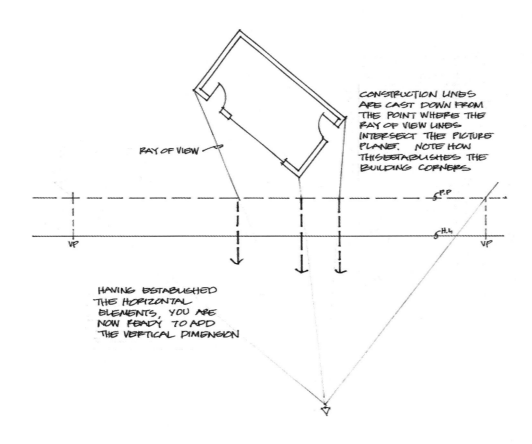

RAY OF VIEW

CONSTRUCTION LINES ARE CAST DOWN FROM THE POINT WHERE THE RAY OF VIEW LINES INTERSECT THE PICTURE PLANE. NOTE HOW THIS ESTABLISHES THE BUILDING CORNERS

P.P

H.L

VP   VP

HAVING ESTABLISHED THE HORIZONTAL ELEMENTS, YOU ARE NOW READY TO ADD THE VERTICAL DIMENSION

Casting Rays: Step 6 – Vertical Story Pole

Now you have a few vertical lines drawn based on the previous step. You do not know, however, how tall the lines should be.

The sketch below is from a vertical reference plane rather than a horizontal one (i.e., plan view) which is what all the previous steps have been based on. Take a few minutes to study and think about the information presented in the sketch below.

Looking back at Step 1, you can see the same vertical reference points identified (i.e., window sill, top of wall, etc.) as are also identified in the sketch shown below.

The location of this vertical line relative to the *Horizon Line* is more of a personal preference. If the entire vertical line were below the *Horizon Line* you would have a *Bird's Eye* view; if the line were completely above the *Horizon Line* it would be a *Worm's Eye* view. Finally, if the vertical line generally straddles the *Horizon Line*, then it is closest to a *Human's Eye* view perspective which is the most often employed type of perspective.

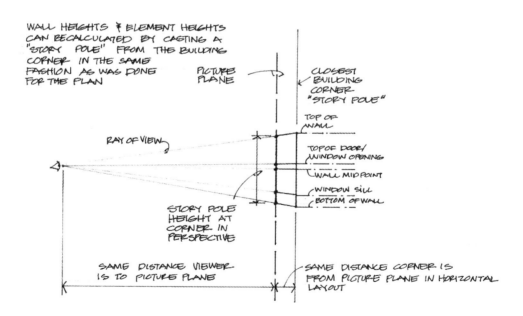

Casting Rays: Step 7 – Connect the dots... Finished!

In this final step you connect the dots and use the same logic to locate the various other features such as windows and doors. As you can see in the sketch below, the end result is a dimensionally and proportionately accurate perspective view of your building.

You can continue to develop and embellish this drawing, or better yet you can use tracing paper and use this crisp line drawing as a reference for a nice free-hand sketch where you then add "props" and maybe shadows.

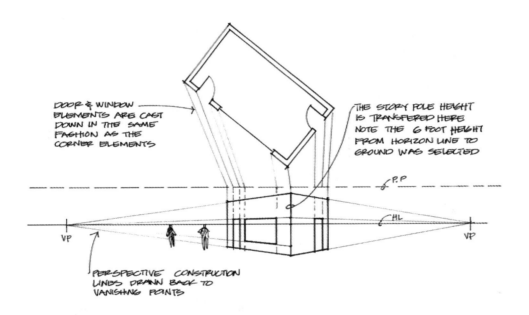

In conclusion to the *Casting Rays* method, you should be able to appreciate how this discussion can help you better understand the "mechanics" of a perspective. Most seasoned designers understand this and are able to better utilize the other, quicker techniques covered in this textbook. So if this did not make sense, especially after doing the exercises, read though the steps again until you understand.

TWO HARBORS HIGH SCHOOL   8602   DWB

Design Study Sketch by *Darryl Booker*,
Associate Professor, North Dakota State University

Rapson Method – Part I

The next method you will be exposed to has been affectionately named after one of co-author McNeill's mentors… **Ralph Rapson** (1914 – 2008).

Mr. Rapson was Dean of the University of Minnesota's School of Architecture for 30 years ('54-'84) and designed many significant buildings as well as furniture. His style was mostly Modernist and included buildings such as the original *Guthrie Theater* (which was demolished in 2006) in Minneapolis, MN as well several US Embassies in Denmark and Sweden. In addition to all these, and many more, accomplishments

Mr. Rapson was a very talented sketcher, and a book was published sharing his work: **Ralph Rapson: Sketches and Drawings from Around the World** (ISBN 978-1890434496). This book would be complimentary to this volume – hundreds of examples and detailed instruction, respectively.

The main steps here involve a quick, loose free-hand sketch, corrective lines with the aid of a straight edge, and then a free-hand sketch utilizing tracing paper. The end result is a very clean looking, surprisingly accurate, freehand style drawing.

Rapson Method: Step 1 – Horizon and Person

The first step to using the *Rapson Method* is like most others – lay down the *Horizon Line* and add the 6′-0″ person for scale. **Remember to move quickly –** you will benefit more by many quick sketches than one detailed sketch.

HORIZON LINE

6 FOOT
PERSON

Rapson Method: Step 2 – Major Reference Lines

The next step is to add a few light lines from the *Vanishing Points* to help set the basic perspective and vertical lines to establish the building's major corners – you do not need to use a straight edge for this step. You will likely have to come back and add additional reference lines as you are not likely to visualize all the edges at this point, so just focus on the significant faces of the façade.

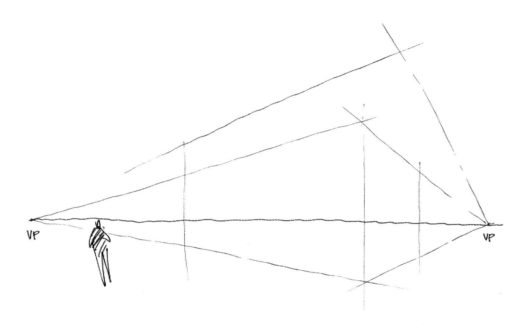

Remember, where you place the vertical lines relative to the *Horizon Lines* has a major impact on the look and feel of the perspective. When you want to see more of the front of the building than the side, then sketch your vertical lines more toward one *Vanishing Point* (as shown above). If you want to see the two sides get equal attention, then place the vertical line which separates the two planes directly in between the two *Vanishing Points*.

Also, you will want to pay attention to the location of the vertical lines relative to the *Horizon Line*. Vertical lines positioned with approximately equal portions above and below the *Horizon Line* create a sense of viewing the building from a person standing within the perspective. This is only true for a smaller building such as the one in this example. A tall building, e.g. a skyscraper, would mostly be above the *Horizon Line*.

Rapson Method: Step 3 – Develop the Idea

With the major reference lines roughed-in, sketch your design idea quickly and with little to no corrections (you will clean things up in the next step). Add enough linework so you feel that all of the major elements are accounted for, such as doors, windows, walls and roof.

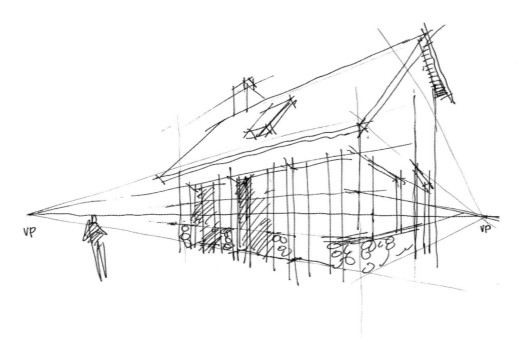

Don't forget: you have your human measuring stick (as previously discussed in this chapter) to help you keep things to scale. Projecting this person onto the building we see that the building is approximately 14'-0" tall. So at this point, if the openings shown were intended to be regular sized doors, you would be way out of proportion. However, that is not the case here as you will see shortly.

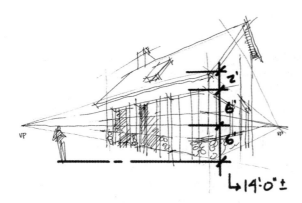

Rapson Method: Step 4 – Firm up the Perspective

The next step here is to firm up the preliminary perspective lines. Up to this point you have just "eye-balled" the sketch to get your ideas on paper. Now you will take a straight edge and "correct" each line. The correction is done by projecting each line back to the *Vanishing Points* and drawing true vertical lines. Some of your lines may be pretty close to accurate while others may be way off.

One trick used to make the following steps a little easier is to draw these corrective lines using a color such as red. You may use a red pencil or pen. Red pens or felt tips work well as they are nice and bold and will show up well in the next step which involves using overlays of paper.

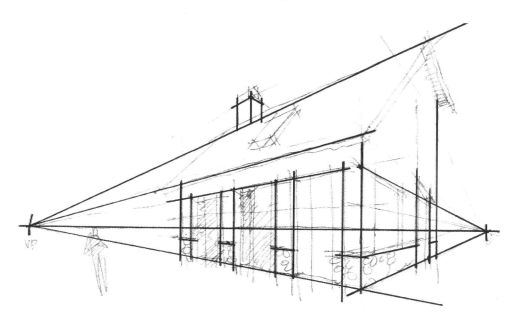

Rapson Method: Step 5 – Final Sketch via an Overlay

This last step involves starting the drawing from scratch. You may be thinking "Whoa, that sounds like a lot of work" and it can be, but the results are worth it; this is why you don't want to add too much detail in the previous steps.

Now that you have the major elements of the building developed and corrected for proper perspective, you take a piece of tracing paper (aka, Bum-Wad) and free-hand sketch or trace over it. You may want to tape the papers to the table to keep things from sliding around on you. **FYI**: Make sure you use drafting tape which, like painters tape, is easily removed!

The end result is a very clean looking free-hand style sketch. It would otherwise be difficult to create a sketch with a free-hand look and be this accurate as far as perspective is concerned. The base drawing, created in the previous steps, is also useful in trying out slight variations on your original ideas!

Rapson Method – Part II

The previous example, which used the *Rapson Method*, had more of a ground level vantage point. This page, and the next two, will walk you through the same process but from a bird's eye view. Most designers prefer the ground level perspective because this is how the building will most often be viewed by people. Occasionally there might be some unique feature about the building which necessitates a bird's eye view, but it is not the most common type of perspective.

Developing a sketch using the *Rapson Method* involves these basic steps:

- Rough free-hand sketch to get the idea down on paper (see image below);
- Firm up the perspective, correcting the rough sketch as required (next page – note the image has been rotated);
- Final sketch via an overlay, using vellum or tracing paper (third page).

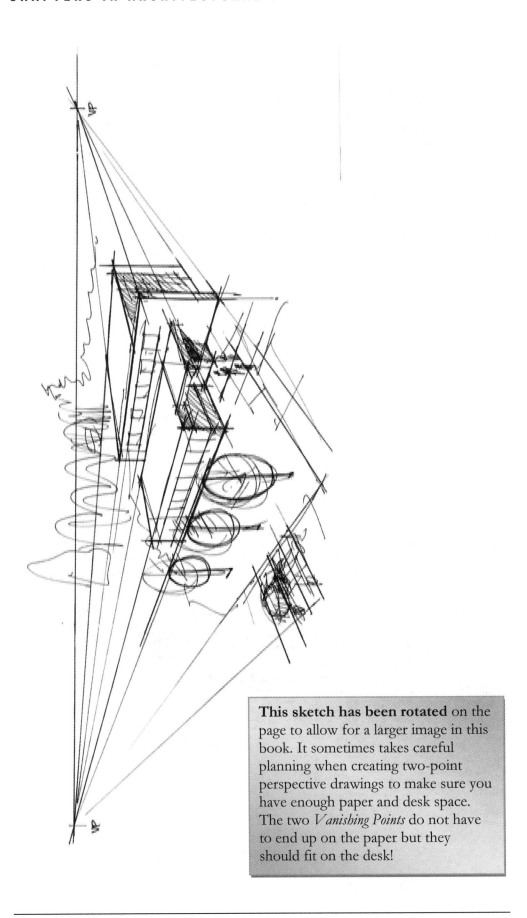

This sketch has been rotated on the page to allow for a larger image in this book. It sometimes takes careful planning when creating two-point perspective drawings to make sure you have enough paper and desk space. The two *Vanishing Points* do not have to end up on the paper but they should fit on the desk!

The image below is a finalized bird's eye perspective sketch using the *Rapson Method.* Adding a box around the image helps to "frame the piece".

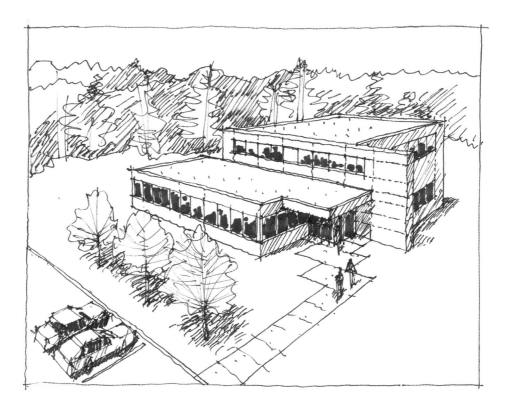

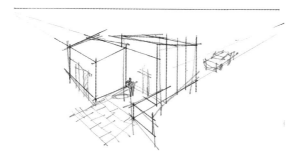

The three sketches (to the left and below) are additional examples of the process just reviewed. Just be aware that not every sketch needs to be perfect; you can correct and refine them later if you like the design enough.

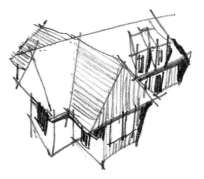

Sketching two-point interior perspectives

The process of creating two-point exterior perspectives can easily be applied to creating interior perspectives. **NOTE**: The distance between the *Vanishing Points* (*VP.1* and *VP.2*) will determine how close, or far away, and how distorted the perspective will be. Also, by making the interior perspective somewhat symmetrical about the horizon (meaning an equal portion of the drawing exists both above and below the HL), the drawing will feel like you are standing within the image and not as if you where in an airplane or as an ant!

The perspective below is of the small portion of floor plan shown below. Notice how the wall with the window does not align with the wall of the smaller room beyond.

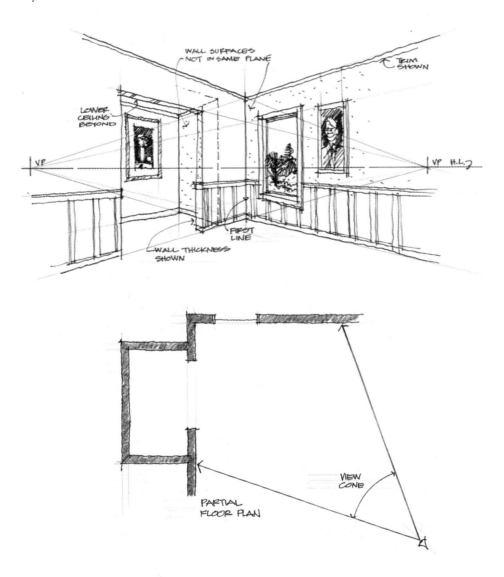

NAME_____ DATE_____

Exercise 9-1

Casting Rays

Complete this perspective using the *Casting Rays* method. The "plane of view" has been placed on the building corner to simplify development of the vertical heights.

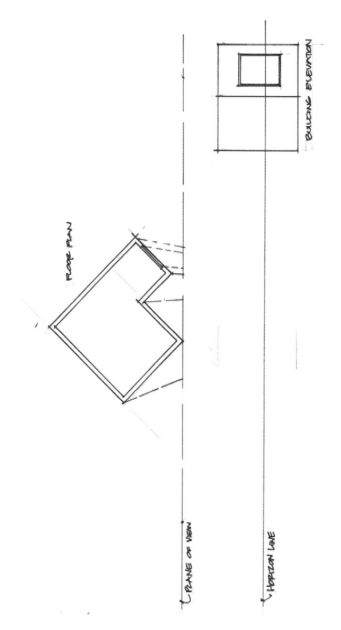

~blank page~

NAME_____ DATE_____

Exercise 9-2

Rapson Method: Correct Perspective

Find the *Horizon Line* and the two *Vanishing Points*. Firm-up the perspective lines using a straightedge; also straighten the vertical lines using a triangle and parallel bar or T-square. You will find it helpful to tape extra paper to this sheet, onto which you may draw the vanishing points and horizon line.

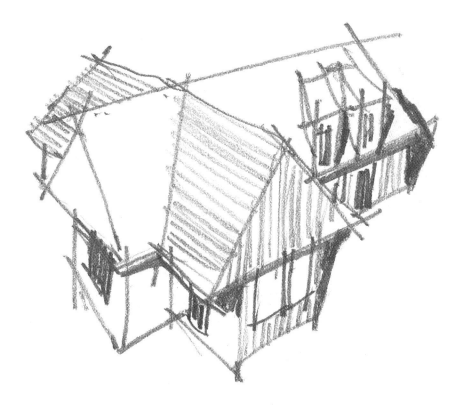

~blank page~

NAME_____DATE_____

Exercise 9-3

Rapson Method: Final Step

The image below has the perspective corrected and is ready for you to add doors windows and other embellishments to get your design ideas across to your client.

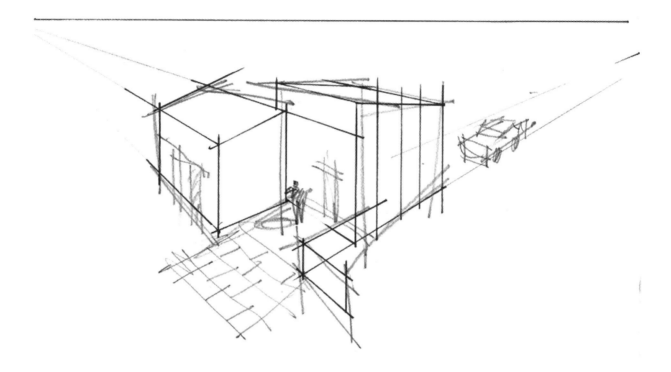

~blank page~

NAME_____ DATE_____

Exercise 9-4

Interior Two-Point Perspective

Select one of these partial plans and sketch an interior two-point perspective of it.

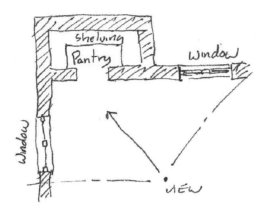
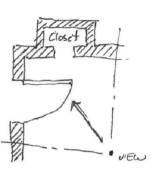

~blank page~

NAME_____DATE_____

Self-Exam:
The following questions can be used as a way to check your knowledge of this lesson. The answers can be found at the lower left on this page.

1. Drawing 2-point interior perspectives is more difficult than 2-point exterior perspectives. (T/F)

2. When repeating a space you first sketch an "X". (T/F)

3. Placement of the *Vanishing Point* has a major impact on the look and feel of the perspective. (T/F)

4. The first step in the *Rapson Method* is to lay down a *Horizon Line* and add a 6'-0" tall person. (T/F)

5. For an interior 2-point perspective, the drawing will feel like the viewer is standing within the room when most of the image is above the *H.I.* (T/F)

Review Questions:
The following questions may be assigned by your instructor as a way to assess your knowledge of this section. Your instructor has the answers to the review questions.

1. Many designers are missing an opportunity when skipping hand sketching and diving right into using the computer. (T/F)

2. With the *Rapson Method* you start out with free hand sketching, then use a straightedge, and then finish by free hand sketching again. (T/F)

3. _____ _____ designed several U.S Embassies.

4. Most designers use the *Casting Rays* method. (T/F)

5. In step 4 of the *Rapson Method* you use a straightedge to firm up the major perspective lines. (T/F)

6. In the _____ _____ method you project lines from the 2D drawings to accurately locate things in the perspective drawings.

7. The *Vanishing Points* are irrelevant when repeating spaces in perspective. (T/F)

8. The Rapson Method is a way in which materials can be shaded to look more realistic. (T/F)

Self-Exam Answers:
1 - F, 2 - T, 3 - T, 4 - T, 5 – F

~blank page~

The Perspective: One-Point

The dramatic one-point perspective is introduced in this chapter. The person viewing a one-point perspective often has a sense of being immersed in the image. As with the two-point perspective drawing type, the one-point represents a real-life representation from a specific vantage point – stay tuned and learn all about it!

Now that you have taken a look at sketching two-point perspectives you will now shift your attention to developing one-point perspectives. A number of the concepts covered in the development study of two-point perspectives also apply to one-point, so it would be helpful if you have previously studied that section of this text.

The sketch below shows a simple example of a one-point perspective. The partial floor plan sketch beside the perspective is the basis of the sketch. Using this technique, you can quickly create a sketch that helps you to visualize the space three-dimensionally. From here you might adjust the floor plans or add color and present it to your client for their approval.

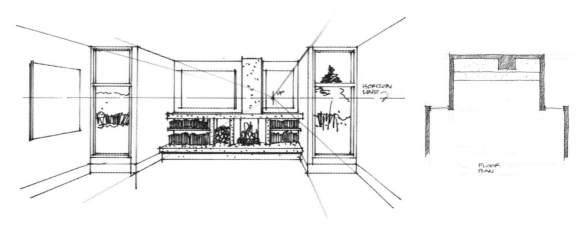

The next two paragraphs introduce two techniques covered in this chapter.

The basic components of a one-point perspective

The process of creating a one-point perspective will be prescribed first in this chapter. The mechanics are very simple and do not take much time to master. Like anything, it just takes practice.

Establishing depth in your perspective

Another topic to be presented is developing a three-dimensional grid which can be used to more accurately sketch items in perspective (in terms of depth from the viewer). This is a very rigid process and often only used for more formal presentation drawings. Note that the location of the Diagonal Point (DP) will establish the depth of the view; when positioned correctly, the view will have the proper feelings of scale and proportion.

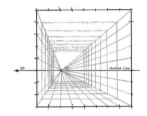

Understanding One-Point Perspectives

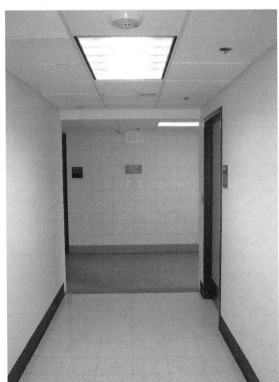

The photo to the left shows a hallway which should help you see how a one-point perspective relates to the real world.

Below is the same image with the *Vanishing Point* discovered; which was done by projecting the perspective lines until they converge with a straight edge.

Vanishing Point lines derived from a photo...

Notice the one-point perspective has three types of lines (with few exceptions):
1. Perspective lines
2. Vertical lines
3. Horizontal lines

The sketch below is formatted in a similar fashion to one previously presented in the two-point perspective chapter. As you can see, however, the circle does not really define a point of distortion for one-point drawings. Again, items completely above the *Horizon Line* are as seen from a "worm's eye" perspective and below the *Horizon Line* as seen from a "bird's eye" view.

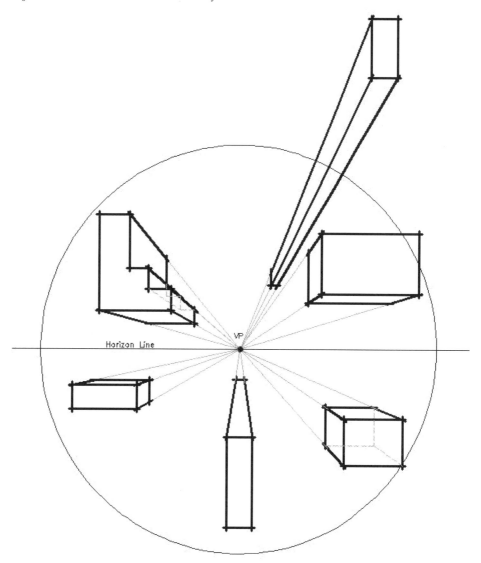

The next two pages provide step-by-step instructions on setting up a one-point perspective and establishing a grid which allows proper proportions and scale to be achieved.

Step A:
Start with a proportionally accurate outline of the space – walls, floor and ceiling.

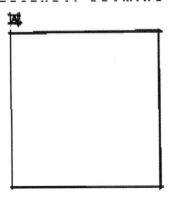
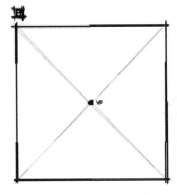

Step B:
Locate the *Vanishing Point* (VP) in a location that will best depict your design. Next, add the four vanishing lines as shown.

Step C:
Sketch the bottom horizontal line; this line will determine the depth of the space. Now you can project the vertical lines up and then add the top horizontal line.

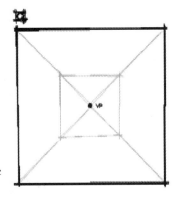
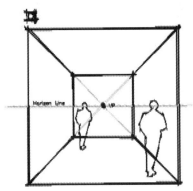

Step D:
Darken the lines which define the space. People are often added to instill a sense of scale; notice how the heads align at the horizon.

Step A:
Same as step 'A' above.

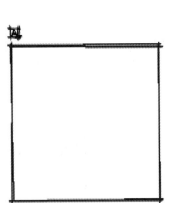
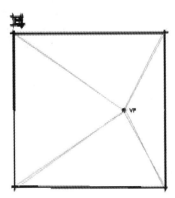

Step B:
Locating the VP to the right can help to direct focus to the left– maybe you have some built-in cabinets on that wall!

Step C:
Same as step 'C' above.

Step D:
Same as step 'D' above.

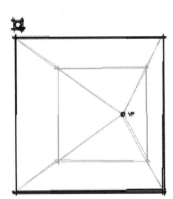
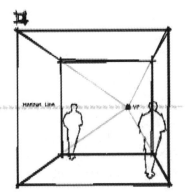

This page shows you how to more accurately establish depth in your sketch. Note the *Diagonal Point's* (DP) placement has an impact on the look and feel of the drawing. You may have to experiment to achieve desired results.

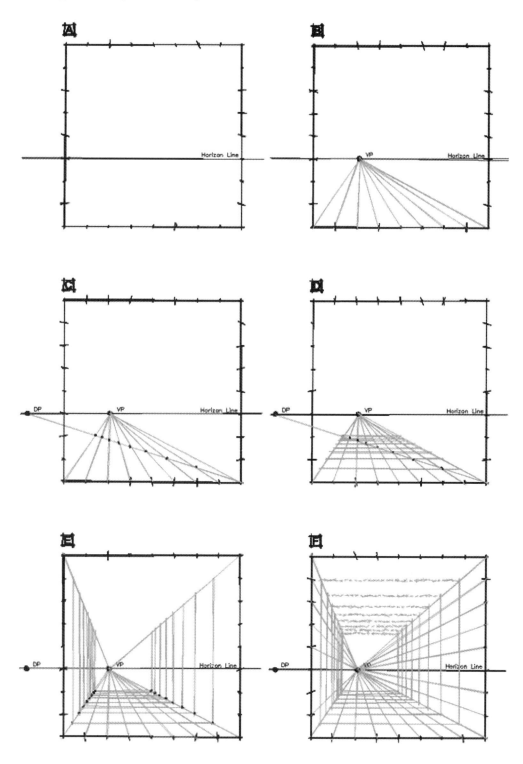

Here are two photographs that demonstrate real one-point perspectives. Keep in mind that perspective drawings are meant to simulate reality.

Now that you have the basics down regarding one-point perspectives, you can apply those techniques plus a few things learned in previous chapters to create a one-point section/interior elevation based on the floor plan below.

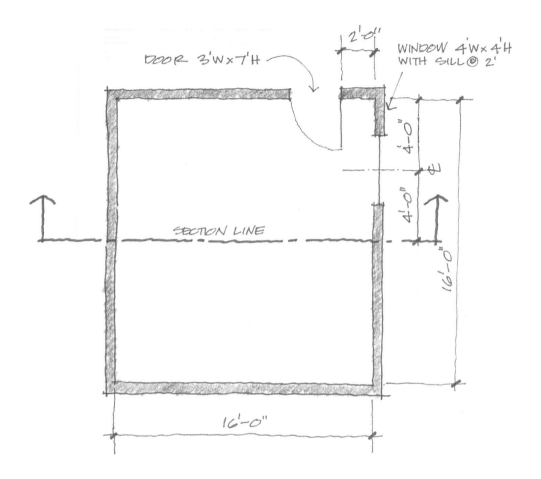

First you start with a section which has been drawn to scale…

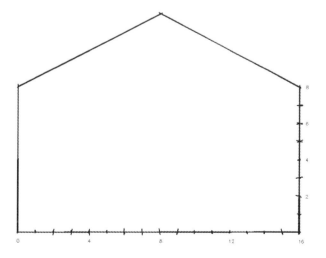

Developing a one-point perspective

Read though the following steps and then try them with the "starter" image in the exercise section following this chapter.

1. Sketch the five perspective lines – from VP to corners.
2. Add the horizontal line – its location will define the depth of the space.
3. Sketch two vertical lines.
4. Locate the center of the back wall with a perspective line, and then add a vertical line up to the ridge line.
5. Connect-the-dots: add the last two sloped lines at the back edge of the roof.

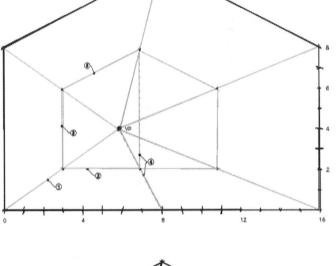

In this exercise, everything drawn at the Cut Plane is to scale, both vertically and horizontally.

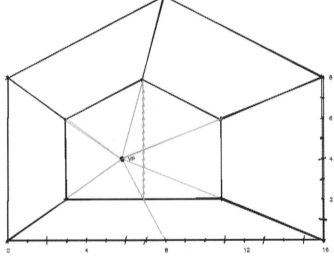

1. [See floor plan on previous page.] Sketch perspective lines to define door width and location.
2. Locate height on adjacent wall.
3. Then project over onto back wall.
4. Add vertical lines as shown.

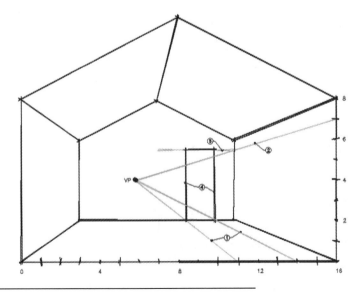

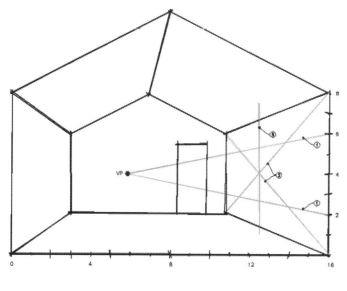

Now you will add a pair of windows to the east wall:

1. Add the two perspective lines to determine the window head and sill locations.
2. Sketch an 'X' to find the center of the wall.
3. Add a vertical line at center of wall.

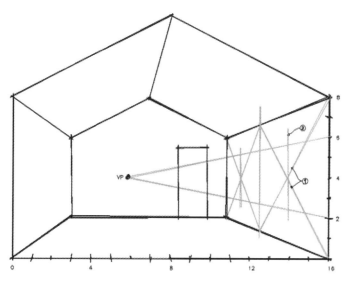

You know the window is 4′ wide and the wall in this view is 8′ wide (see plan view on previous page), thus you can divide the spaces as previously covered:

1. Sketch 'X's in the two spaces.
2. Add a vertical line at the intersection of each 'X'.
3. You now have the extents of the window defined and can be darkened for clarity.

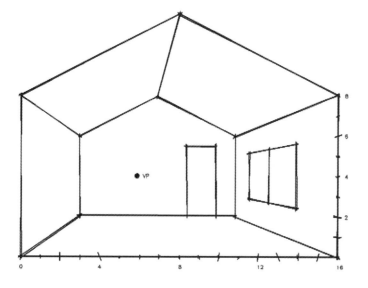

The final step is to darken the major lines and add embellishments, like window and door trim, wall's base, etc.

You will get a chance to practice this in the end of chapter exercises.

Once you have learned to create one-point interior elevations, you can easily apply that technique to creating one-point floor plans. This type of perspective drawing allows you to quickly think about the design of an entire room, rather than just one corner (i.e., two walls).

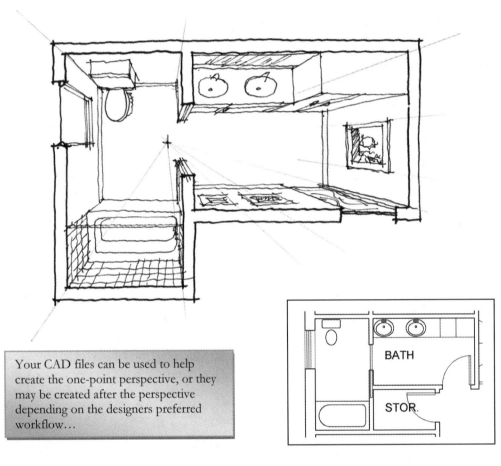

Your CAD files can be used to help create the one-point perspective, or they may be created after the perspective depending on the designers preferred workflow...

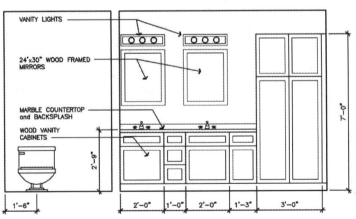

Simply sketch the footprint of the room, pick a *Vanishing Point* (VP) and then project the walls up and add features. See the next page for examples on various VP locations and how they affect the resultant perspective.

BATH

STOR.

VANITY LIGHTS

24"x30" WOOD FRAMED MIRRORS

MARBLE COUNTERTOP and BACKSPLASH

WOOD VANITY CABINETS

7'-0"

2'-9"

1'-6"   2'-0"   1'-0"   2'-0"   1'-3"   3'-0"

Plan or Elevation and VP location...

You need to think about the information you want to convey in your one-point perspective before you start drawing. Without thinking through to your desired result, you could find you have wasted a lot of time if you get started too quickly. If you want to highlight a lot of detail on the wall then you should do a perspective from an elevation vantage point. If you want to show overall relationships and circulation you could create a plan-type perspective.

In the example below you see a rough sketch of a kitchen floor plan (on the left) and (3) plan-type and (3) elevation-type one-point perspectives. Notice the various *Vanishing Point* (VP) locations and what they show and don't show.

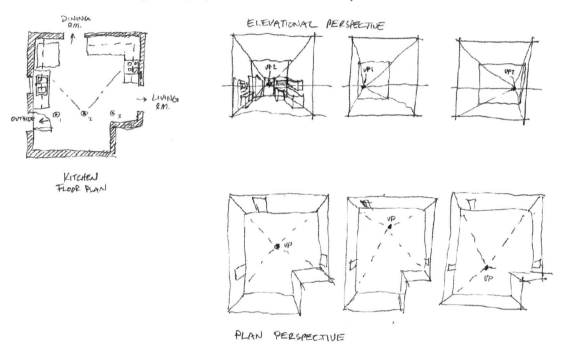

PLAN PERSPECTIVE

The 1-point sketch to the left is a field sketch of a restaurant in Europe. Notice this one-point perspective captures the essence of the space with minimal detail: the forms in the ceilings, the shape of the chair backs, the layout of the tables, the quantity and location of light fixtures.

Below is an example of the melding of a digital CAD drawing and a hand sketch. Simply print out a floor plan or building section, lay a piece of tracing paper over and begin producing a one-point perspective. Picking the *Vanishing Point* is very important – you want to make sure no major features are hidden. Once the *Vanishing Point* has been established, you can then project lines from the VP through the various corners within the floor plan. The first line you draw to represent the top-of-wall will dictate all others via the "connect-the-dots" process.

This concept even works for 3D programs such as Revit Architecture. You can print out an exterior perspective of the building and then hand sketch various siding and window options quickly without having to meticulously lay out each in an exacting computer program.

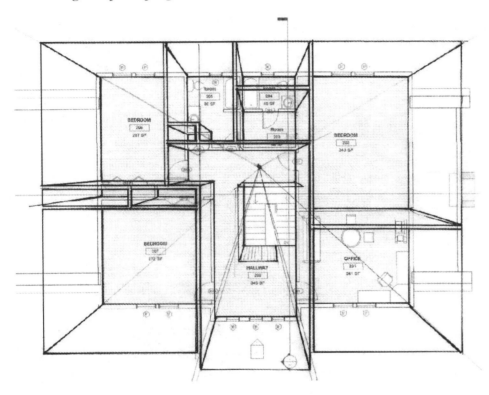

The image below is an example of a student's work using one-point perspective drawings to convey design intent. These sketches have been assembled onto a foam-core board to facilitate a presentation, in which case the board is placed on an easel. Most of the time, these days, a digital projector and Microsoft PowerPoint would be used to streamline the process and allow for much larger images to be displayed for the client.

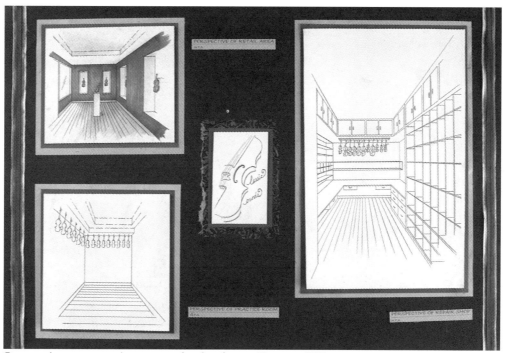

One-point perspective examples by **Anne Porter** CID

Three-Point Perspective

Just as the two-point perspective is generally more realistic than the one-point perspective, there is a third *Vanishing Point* that occurs in most settings. The third *Vanishing Point* can be above or below the object being viewed. As you will see on the next page, the 3rd VP is below the object when the object is being viewed from above – and vice-versa when viewed from a worm's eye view.

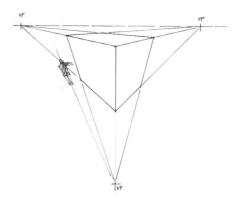

Many architectural perspective drawings omit the third *Vanishing Point* to simplify the process and to remove the slight distortion that would otherwise distract from the main intent of the piece; which is to convey design intent. Rather than a third

Vanishing Point, all lines which would normally be defined by the 3rd VP are drawn vertical. This is done with a parallel bar (or T-Square) and a 90 degree triangle.

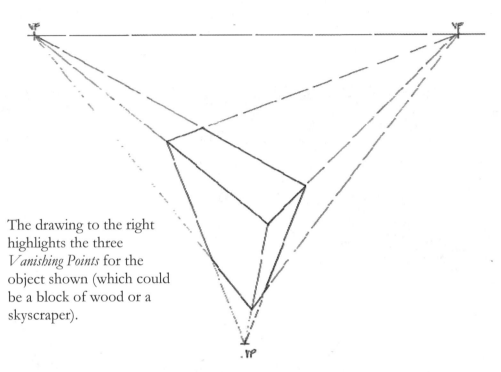

The drawing to the right highlights the three *Vanishing Points* for the object shown (which could be a block of wood or a skyscraper).

Below is a photo demonstrating a 3-point perspective. The smaller image to the right reveals the third *Vanishing Point*. When the object is viewed from below, the 3rd VP is above. Note: this photo is slightly distorted due to the camera lens.

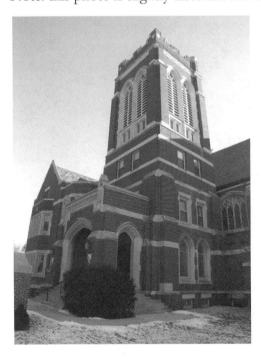

NAME_____DATE_____

Exercise 10-1

One Point Perspective

Use the image below as a starting point to create the same perspective as covered on the previous pages. Don't forget to make a few copies if you think you might need a few practice runs. Include the following aspects in your design:

1. Add a *Vanishing Point* (VP) more to the right to create a unique view.

2. Add the door and window per the examples above and the floor plan.

3. Also add the following items:
   a. 2'x4' skylight.
   b. Add 3 cabinets to the left wall (2'-0"x2'-0"x3'-0" high).
   c. Sketch a 4'x8' rug centered on the room.

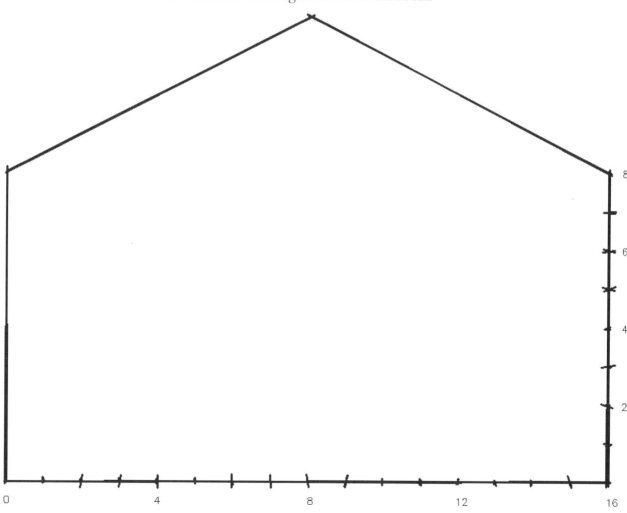

~blank page~

NAME_____DATE_____

Exercise 10-2

Discover the Vanishing Point

Use a heavy black marker and a straightedge to discover the vanishing point.

~blank page~

NAME_____DATE_____

Exercise 10-3

One-Point Exercise
Create a one point perspective of your initials like the example.

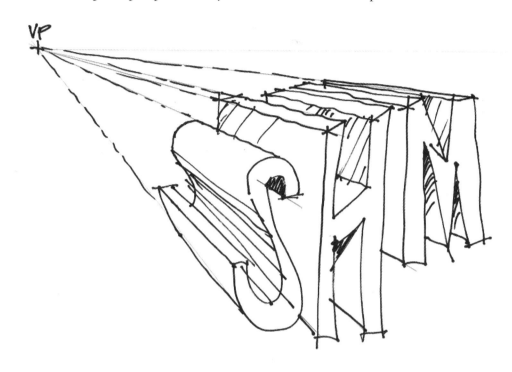

~blank page~

NAME_____ DATE_____

Exercise 10-4

One-Point Exercise

Take this section of a public entry space and create a one-point interior perspective. Pick your own vanishing point on the horizon line. Delineate the interior walls, floors and ceiling as you see fit. You may use a straight edge or "freehand" lines. Get the basic "bones" of the space drawn.

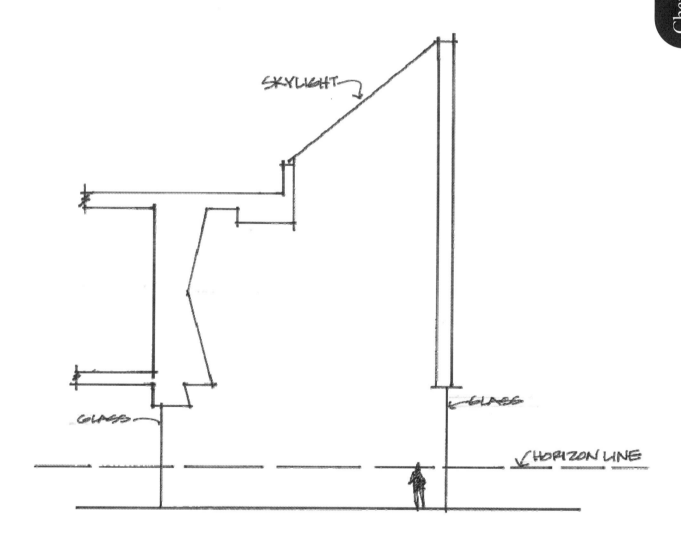

~blank page~

NAME_____ DATE_____

Exercise 10-5

Discover the Third Vanishing Point
Locate the third vanishing point in the photo provided. There is often distortion in photographs due to the camera lens, so you may approximate the point if needed. In any case, the point should be on this page.

~blank page~

NAME_____ DATE_____

Self-Exam:
The following questions can be used as a way to check your knowledge of this lesson. The answers can be found at the lower left on this page.

1. Many architectural drawings omit the third *Vanishing Point*. (T/F)

2. For a one-point (1-point) perspective, you should locate the *Vanishing Point* so no major features are hidden. (T/F)

3. One-point perspectives can be created for floor plans. (T/F)

4. The location of the *Vanishing Point* has a significant impact on the final look of a 1-point perspective drawing. (T/F)

5. It is not possible to find the *Vanishing Point* in a photograph. (T/F)

Review Questions:
The following questions may be assigned by your instructor as a way to assess your knowledge of this section. Your instructor has the answers to the review questions.

1. It is not possible to find the midpoint of a space/surface in a 1-point perspective. (T/F)

2. You can find all three *Vanishing Points* in a photo (by projecting lines back until they converge), but they may be far off the page. (T/F)

3. Once you determine the height of one wall, in a 1-point floor plan, you can start to "connect the dots". (T/F)

4. There are no vertical lines in a 1-point perspective. (T/F)

5. Heads of people align with the *Horizon Line* (for eye-level views). (T/F)

6. _____ _____ is the name of the second "point" in a 1-point perspective, when one needs to accurately establish depth.

7. When the 3rd Vanishing Point is omitted, the perspective lines that would have been defined by it are simply drawn as vertical lines. (T/F)

8. In a 1-point perspective, everything drawn in the cut plane (or main elevation) is to scale. (T/F)

~blank page~

Section Three

Sketching in a Digital World

"You've got to bumble forward into the unknown".
Frank Gehry

Entourage and Reflections

*In the end, buildings are for people, so it makes sense to render
your drawings with people in them. Adding people, trees and other
"props" brings an otherwise stagnant image to life! The use of
reflections in your sketches also adds a layer of realism.*

Adding decent looking people, trees and cars to a sketch can be a little
tricky. This chapter will give you a few tips and tricks to help make the
process more successful for you. Once you have a handle on adding
entourage, reflections, shades and shadows, you will be able to create some
stunning sketches and renderings.

Animal Center perspective sketch by **Duane Thorbeck** FAIA

Adding People

Not only do people help to bring your sketches to life, they also give the viewer a sense of scale – as was previously discussed in the section on "the human measuring stick". The simple sketch of people shown to the right can be created by imagination or you can trace over people in various poses as found in magazines, newspapers or digital photographs. In any case, you want to make sure the people are in the correct perspective and the proper scale. If you are tracing from a periodical or a tracing file you can always scale the image up or down, before tracing it, using a copy machine. Getting the "models" in the correct perspective is not as easy; for example, you cannot trace a person pictured mainly from above in an eye-level rendering.

For eye-level renderings, meaning the angle of the view is as if a person were standing on the ground, the heads of most people will be at the *Horizon Line* no matter where they are in the scene. As you can see in the sketch below, some people are very close while others appear far in the distance, but most of them have their heads aligned with the horizon. The exceptions are when a person is sitting, bending over or just shorter than the person they are standing next to.

EYE LEVEL OF VIEWER

If you are tracing people from a newspaper or a magazine, you should be careful not to get too detailed. In fact, you should simplify and slightly alter the sketch so the person is not recognizable; if you traced a famous person (e.g., Bill Gates) and your sketch looked just like him, you could be setting yourself up for a lawsuit!

Some like to be very figurative with the people and trees they add, leaving the primary focus on the architecture, so they simply draw the outline of the people as shown below. These outlines are often left open inside – even when the area all around them is heavily rendered.

Many designers have a book called **ENTOURAGE: A Tracing File For Architecture and Interior Design Drawing** (by Ernest Burden, McGraw-Hill Professional Publishing). This book has a couple hundred pages of people, cars and trees in various poses which can traced and used in your architectural design sketches.

Adding Trees

Trees can be added in much the same way as people; i.e., imagination or tracing. There are many varieties of trees and seasons to consider; this requires a basic knowledge of trees for the best results.

Don't forget to Watch the Entourage video:
Make sure you take a look at the entourage videos on the DVD that came with this textbook for some great tips on how to actually create trees.

These two pages of trees show a few types and styles of hand sketched trees commonly used in architectural drawings. The use of poché or hatching (or lack of it) can help to indicate fullness or season; just stringy lines with no hatching gives the feel of late fall or winter. Each tree should be slightly different to make the sketch feel more natural – this is pretty easy in a hand sketch as compared to a computer rendering where the same tree is copied around the model.

TIP:
You can keep a folder of magazine and newspaper clippings of people in various poses, cars from various angles and trees. This folder can be your own personal tracing file archive. You can scale them up or down on the photocopy machine as needed to match the proportions of your rendering.

This is one of co-author Steve McNeill's travel sketches showing people, trees, benches, etc., in perspective to make the scene very lively!

Adding Vehicles

Not to sound too redundant, but you can also add vehicles in a similar fashion to that of people and trees. Take a look at the reflections section later in the chapter for tips on how to render the vehicle's glass. These vehicles, shown below, were traced from a newspaper advertisement.

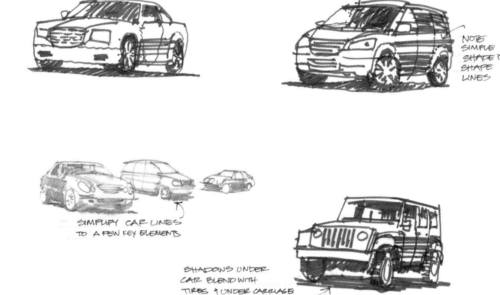

NOTE SIMPLE SHAPE ? SHAPE LINES

SIMPLIFY CAR LINES TO A FEW KEY ELEMENTS

SHADOWS UNDER CAR BLEND WITH TIRES & UNDER CARRIAGE

Consistent Shadows

When adding people, trees and vehicles it is important to decide upfront where the sun is coming from and in which direction the resultant shadows are cast; a good rendering will always be consistent in this respect. It is helpful if you can find examples to trace that have the shadows already matching your rendering, but this is not necessary as you can trace the item and then add shadows separately that work. Using a Light Table (i.e., a table with a glass surface which has lights under the glass to make it easier to see through multiple pieces of paper) is helpful when tracing entourage, but you can also use an exterior window on a sunny day; just tape your pages to the window and trace away!

When you are working on "specialty" renderings – that is, when you need people in specific poses – you may need to use your digital camera and photograph people (likely co-workers). You can then print the picture at the proper scale and trace it. You can also take pictures from several angles to make sure you get the correct perspective to trace.

The sketch above is actually of the authors (Stine standing & McNeill sitting) who posed for a rendering of an assisted living facility.

Notice how the use of reflections in the rendering above makes the floor look shiny like marble or terrazzo. The next section begins a discussion on the techniques for adding reflections to your drawings.

Adding "props" to your sketches is sometimes helpful. Notice the large plant placed in the rendering to the right. To make it more realistic shadows were added to the column and floor!

Reflections

Reflections occur throughout buildings and their settings. The most obvious case of reflection is at water. Buildings and landscape elements reflect images that are in complete perspective mirrored about the surface of the water. The perspective continues below the water plane virtually in the same height it appears above it. The example, shown below, illustrates the height of the building corner is the same below (or on) the water plane.

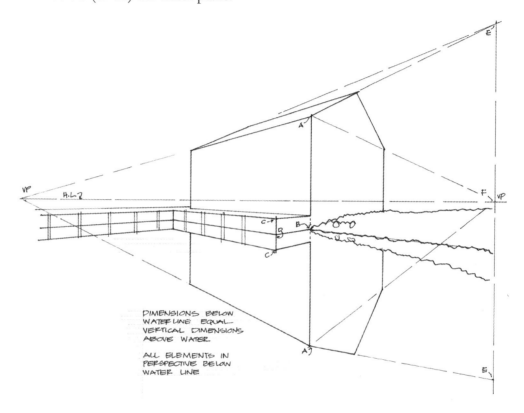

The image above shows, more technically, how reflections are laid out. Before turning the page to see a more refined version of this building, take a felt tipped pen and mark a line along the water's edge in the image above to make sure you understand where it is. The image on the next page serves as an example of how a sketch of the same building would actually look with water reflections. This sketch portrays glass in sunlight with ground level trees, while the water reflects the building, trees and the edge of the water. The surface of the water is often active with subtle waves which can be easily represented by loose horizontal lines used to blur the crisp lines of the mirrored perspective.

This should be clear, but a reflection is a mirrored image and not an image rotated 180 degrees.

Norway Boathouse sketch by **Duane Thorbeck** FAIA

Windows reflect much like water. In the example of the photograph shown below, you see how the upper level of the glass is reflecting the bright blue sky, while the lower level of glass reflects trees and adjacent buildings – which are typically much darker, if not totally black looking.

Just for Fun: Linoleum Block Printing

This has nothing (directly) to do with Entourage or Reflections, but we thought it would be fun to "share" rather than leave this page blank (which would be required to get the next chapter to start in the correct spot).

Linoleum Block Prints create images that use black and white contrast to formulate images. Cutting your own blocks can be a fun way to explore this high contrast imagery that relies on dense tones.

Linoleum Block Printing involves sketching a mirror image design on a smooth piece of linoleum (mounted to a wood block) and then carving the linoleum – leaving your sketch lines untouched (i.e., they remain at the original smooth surface). Next one inks the surface and presses it onto a piece of paper or card front to create images such as the ones shown to the left.

The photo shows an example of two carved blocks and the tools used.

This is a great technique one can use to create greeting and holiday cards – a custom card showing creativity!

NAME_____ DATE_____

Exercise 11-1

Entourage

This is a sample of a highly rendered drawing depicting a landscape plaza garden area with many forms: trees, shrubs, pavements, benches, tables and planted beds. Note the use of shadows to suggest depth. Create a landscaped garden on the back of this page, but use the rendering methods for cars, trees, sidewalks, etc., and indicate shadows to portray depth.

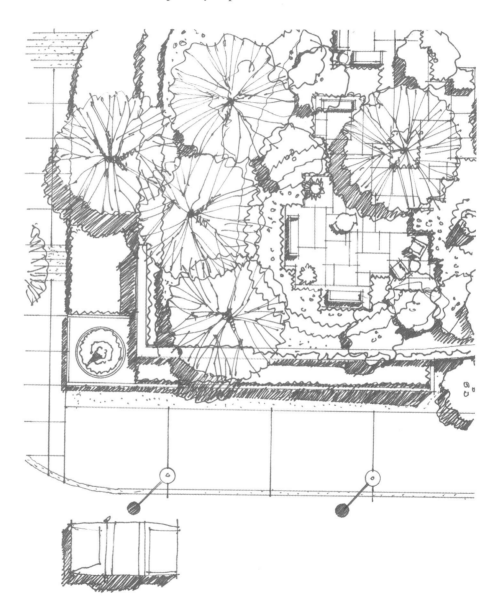

~blank page~

NAME_____ DATE_____

Exercise 11-2

Reflections

Complete the perspective of the waterside building. You may draw it as on a still day or choose to portray water in action.

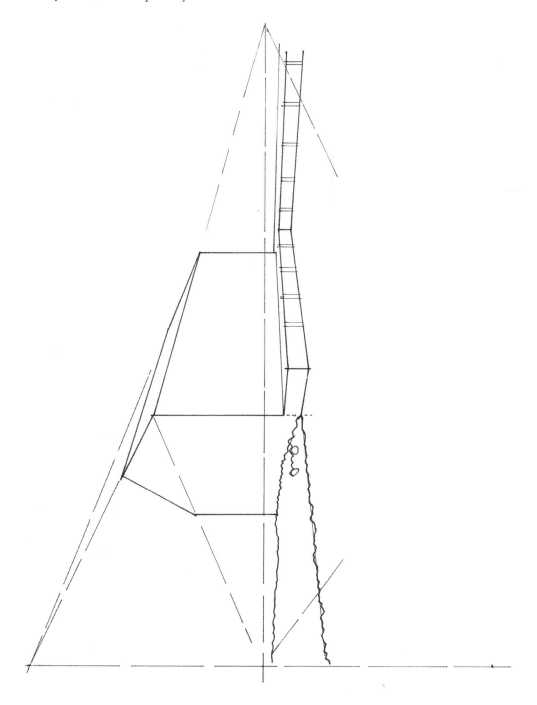

Chapter 11 EXERCISES

~blank page~

NAME_____DATE_____

Exercise 11-3

Reflections

Use the hatching techniques you learned in this book to add the reflections shown in the top photograph in the bottom one.

~blank page~

NAME_____DATE_____

Exercise 11-4

Reflections

Complete the perspective of the waterside boathouse. You may draw it as on a still day or choose to portray water in action. Sketch in reflections of the boat.

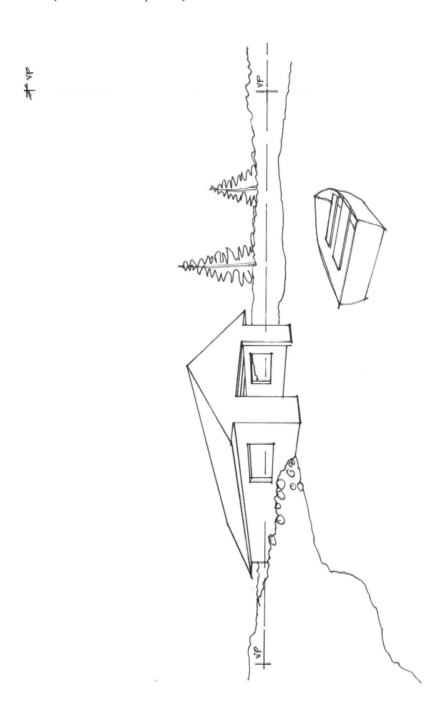

~blank page~

NAME_____ DATE_____

Self-Exam:
The following questions can be used as a way to check your knowledge of this lesson. The answers can be found at the lower left on this page.

1. A reflection is a 180° rotated image. (T/F)

2. Each tree should be sketched exactly the same. (T/F)

3. *Entourage* helps bring life to your design/rendering. (T/F)

4. The DVD, which came with this book, has a tutorial video on *Entourage*. (T/F)

5. For the most part, in an eye-level rendering, is the people's _____ align with the *Horizon Line*.

Review Questions:
The following questions may be assigned by your instructor as a way to assess your knowledge of this section. Your instructor has the answers to the review questions.

1. With glass windows, reflections are rendered lighter colors (for the sky) above and darker colors (for the ground) below. (T/F)

2. When tracing people, shadows should only be traced if they match those in your rendering (i.e., direction/angle relative to the sun). (T/F)

3. It is not possible to imply the season when sketching trees. (T/F)

4. Vehicles are positioned upon a heavy black _____ which blends with the black tires.

5. *Linoleum Block Printing* involves carving a pattern/image, in reverse, out of linoleum which has been mounted to a wood block. (T/F)

6. Some designers like to simply outline people, trees and cars rather than add refining detail which distracts from the building. (T/F)

7. For interior renderings, _____ on the floor can make the floor finish appear to be marble or terrazzo.

8. In a reflection on water, the dimensions below the water line are half the dimensions above. (T/F)

Self-Exam Answers:
1 - F, 2 - F, 3 - T, 4 - T, 5 – head

~blank page~

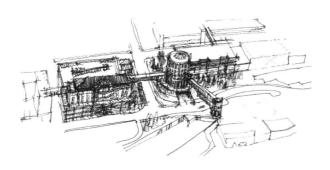

Digital Sketching Techniques

Even though hand sketching is a great tool in and of itself, most designers often find ways to speed the process along. Remember they still have meeting minutes to deal with! This chapter will reveal a few such digital hybrid sketching tricks which may make your task a bit easier.

Every modern design utilizes a computer in one way or another. The trick is determining when to sketch something by hand and when to use the computer. The two extremes are: you spend too much time sketching and have to recreate a significant amount of graphical information in your Computer Aided Design program (CAD; AutoCAD or Revit Architecture, for example) with little time to spare; or you jump right into the CAD program and try to do all your designing there, rather than employing the fluid sketching process which allows for several design iterations, and ultimately gives you the most options and the best design solution. The best scenario is to find the proper balance between the two, CAD and sketching, and in fact they overlap quite a bit.

The subsequent pages will introduce you to a few digital sketching techniques utilized by co-author McNeill regularly on real-world projects. Just to make it clear, you will not be required to use a computer or any software in this textbook. The exercises will try to explain the process at a high level, rather than step-by-step, so you understand what can be done. Additionally, the exercises will have the "digital" base-work done and then you do the sketching part.

Machu Picchu by
Duane Thorbeck FAIA

Photographic Fako-Blendo

As you have previously studied, and perhaps already knew, a perspective drawing mimics what is seen by the human eye. Photographs also capture the perspective qualities we see, so with a digital camera you can snap several pictures of an existing building or interior space as the basis for a perspective sketch. This works great for additions and remodelings, as well as being the springboard for ideas on a totally new project. An example of each will be presented for your enjoyment!

Interior One-Point Perspective

In this example you may have an existing space, a computer lab shown, which you want to remodel. Or, maybe you are developing drawings for a new building but have a collection of photographs and one or two have the look and feel you are generally going after in your design. In either case, you can use the following process to quickly develop a great looking sketch with a minimum of time and effort:

Step-by-step process:

1. Take a picture with a digital camera.
2. Print the photograph as large as possible on 11″x17″ paper.
3. Tape the photo to your drawing board.
4. Tape a fresh piece of tracing paper on top of the photo.
5. Discover the *Vanishing Point* by projecting lines from the picture back.
6. Hand trace the major elements you wish to retain in the photo.
7. Embellish the sketch with new ideas; this example shows the ceiling raised, indirect lighting and exterior windows added.

Exterior Two-Point

Perspective

Another way in which to apply the *Photographic Fako-Blendo* technique (**FYI**: Fako-Blendo is a made-up word, incase you were wondering) is on an exterior perspective. Just like the previous interior example, this could be utilized on both new and remodel building projects. The example below (and continued on the next two pages) shows how you can use this method to delineate the design of a new building based on an existing, similarly proportioned building.

Below you see the photo of the building used as the underlay, and below it you see the end result. The next two pages show the intermediate step to this process.

This intermediate step, which has been expanded across two pages to show more detail, reveals some of the preliminary work required to modify the building pictured. First, the two *Vanishing Points* were discovered by projecting lines back until they all intersect at two points. Next you "connect the dots" between the two *Vanishing Points* to document the *Horizon Line*.

Once you have the *Vanishing Points* located, you can use them to add new elements to the sketch such as the cross-gable shown roughed in here. Note that the *Vanishing Points* do not need to be in the picture (as you can see in the refined sketch on the previous page), but they do need to fit on your desk (or your neighbor's desk); so make sure you plan accordingly!

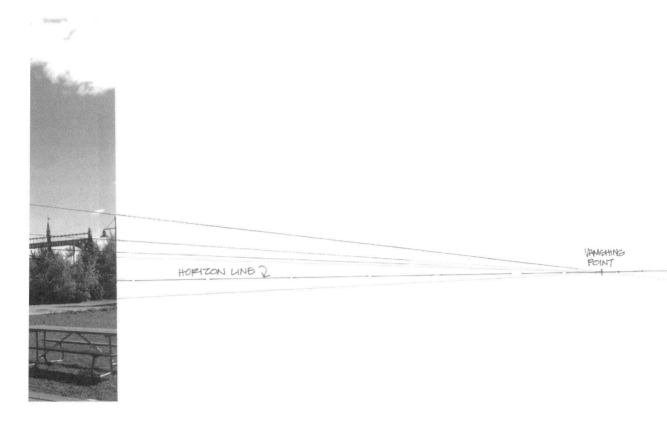

Don't just copy it…

One point we would like to make clear is that we are not, in any way, suggesting you directly copy or plagiarize anyone's work. Rather, the main idea is that you see a space or building, and you can visualize your design generally fitting that mold. From there you rework the "clay" until you are happy with the outcome, which usually does not look too much like the original (of course classrooms only vary so much, but our example is still quite different).

This workflow is not too far removed from common practice in which an architect looks through several magazines and marks pages that catch the eye. Then the pages may be attached to a board and referenced from time-to-time during the design for inspiration.

Digital Camera Photograph Perspective

The images below represent a visual introduction to the *Digital Camera Photograph Perspective* process which will be explained in more detail starting on the next page.

1. CAD
Drawing

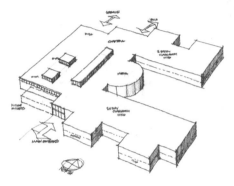

4. Sketch Overlay: Option "A"

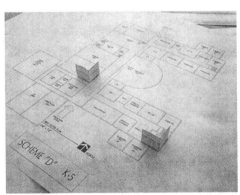

2. Photo of CAD Drawing

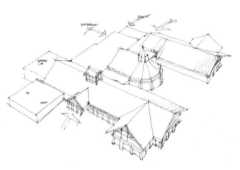

5. Sketch Overlay: Option "B"

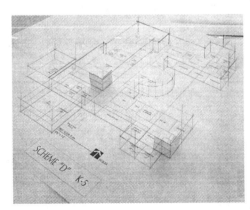

3. Sketching on Printout of Photo

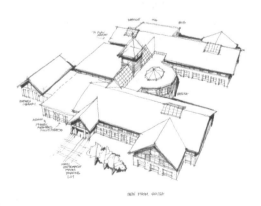

6. Sketch Overlay: Option "C"

Digital Camera Photograph Perspective

This is one of co-author McNeill's favorite perspective methods simply because it is fast, accurate in perspective and allows for the building and site to be depicted together. The process starts with a building floor plan (the ground level) or site plan (see sketch below). This plan is taped onto a table; vertical elements such as wood blocks, cardboard, etc., are positioned to act as "story poles" by which one can judge heights. Next, pictures are taken using a digital camera (see example on the next page). You can select many different vantage points and angles to best portray the project.

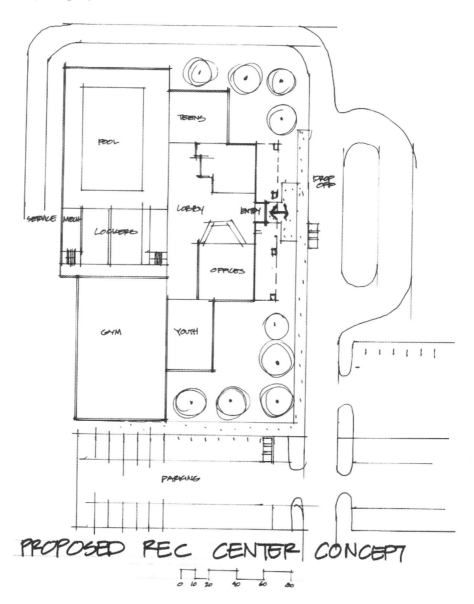

Once you have selected an image, it can be sent to a printer or plotter and enlarged to create a drawing background; 11″x17″ paper is a common/convenient size.

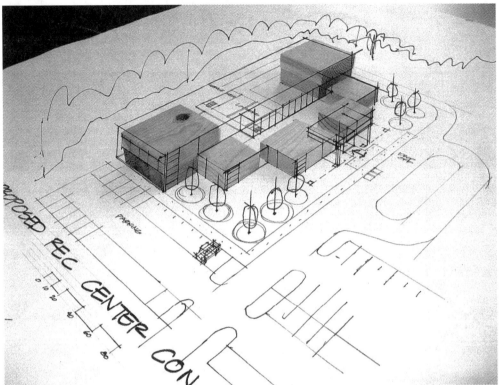

Digital photograph taken of a 2D site plan; wood blocks added to establish height.

The image is drawn upon to establish the major building forms, typically in block fashion. You will note that there is no *Vanishing Point* or *Horizon Line* to guide your perspective lines. Rather you will find lines in perspective that are from other site or building elements that guide your perspective lines to an accurate angle. The vertical wall elements will portray the third *Vanishing Point* direction into the ground. You may wish to follow this angling or simply draft the walls as if all are vertical and parallel to each other for simplicity (this is the most common option used).

Any number of sketch and drawing types can then be produced over this base with tracing paper. For example, quick studies drawn with thick felt-tipped pens or delicate renderings for presentation. Take a minute and note how the three designs (shown on the next two pages) relate to the base drawing (shown above).

Design options developed on base-photo shown on the previous page.

FAT FELT TIP
MASSING
STUDY

"V" ROOF STUDY

Once you find a design that you like, or you think the client might like, you can then sketch a more refined drawing based on the more loosely drawn overlays shown on the previous page (i.e., they are not meant to be presentation drawings). Sometimes the studious designer will develop, to a point, two or more designs to show the client. These options may be:

- The design the architect likes best
- The design the architect thinks the client will like best
- The design option which costs less to build

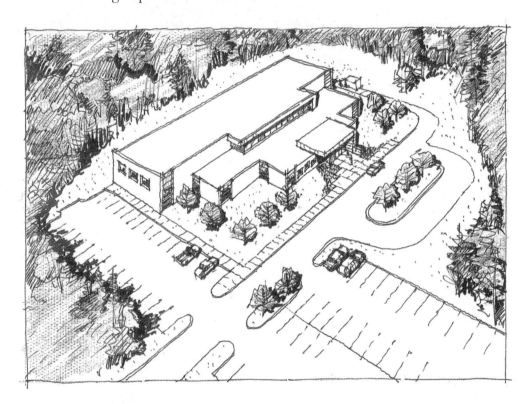

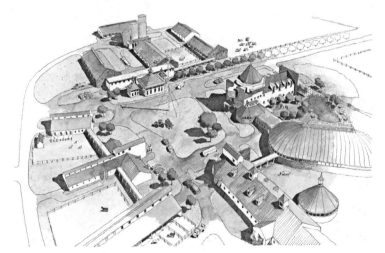

The sketch to the left was not necessarily drawn using the method just described but it could have been. Imagine a photo taken of the campus site plan from this sketch's vantage point.

Hershey Farm Discovery sketch by **Duane Thorbeck** FAIA

NAME_____ DATE_____

Exercise 12-1

Digital Camera Photograph Perspective; *page 1 of 2*

In this exercise you will draw a farmstead. The site plan as shown here has been
attached to a table and an oblique bird's-eye type image has been made for your
use (using a digital camera and printer). Be creative and sketch in the type of barn
and house in your design. Estimate the building heights by eye. Sketch in some
light vertical guidelines at the building's corners and then horizontal (i.e.,
perspective) lines. Sketch in trees, fences and other landscape elements.

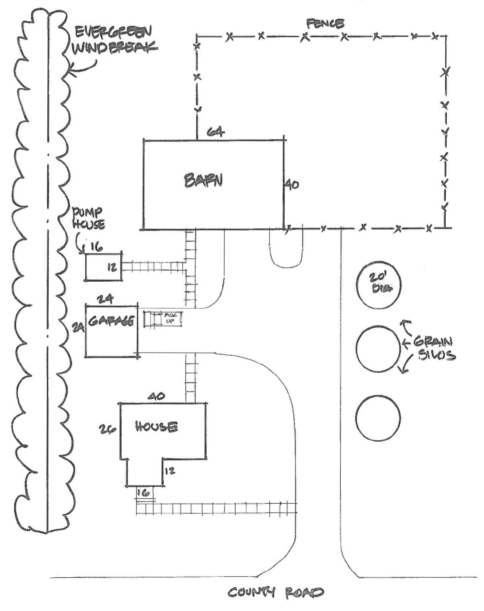

~blank page~

NAME_____ DATE_____

Exercise 12-1 (continued)

Digital Camera Photograph Perspective; *page 2 of 2*
Use this photograph of the site plan shown on the previous page to develop your perspective of the farmstead; the photo has been rotated 90 degrees for size.

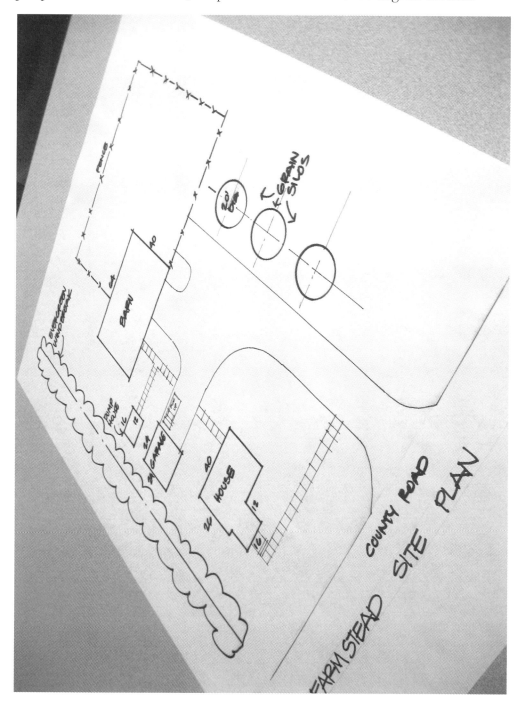

~blank page~

NAME_____DATE_____

Exercise 12-2

Digital Camera Photograph Perspective

Create the same image from this chapter but at the angle shown below.

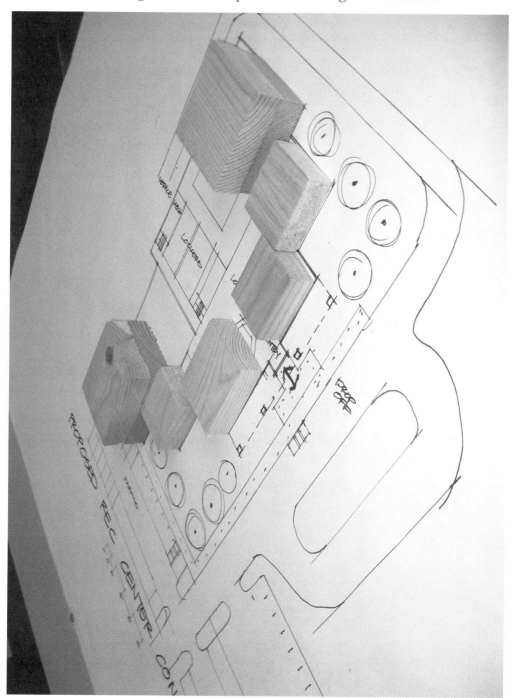

~blank page~

NAME_____ DATE_____

Exercise 12-3

Photographic Fako-Blendo

Using the Fako-Blendo techniques, add a symmetrical addition.

Chapter **12 EXERCISES**

~blank page~

NAME_____ DATE_____

Self-Exam:

The following questions can be used as a way to check your knowledge of this lesson. The answers can be found at the lower left on this page.

1. Every design utilizes a computer in some way. (T/F)

2. In the Photographic Facko-Blendo method, you will occasionally need to "discover" the *Vanishing Point* in order to add major elements. (T/F)

3. Tracing paper is an important part of the techniques shown in this chapter. (T/F)

4. It's okay to copy (or plagiarize) the design of another building. (T/F)

5. On a remodeling project, you could sketch over a _____.

Review Questions:

The following questions may be assigned by your instructor as a way to assess your knowledge of this section. Your instructor has the answers to the review questions.

1. Architects often look at magazines to get ideas from other designs. (T/F)

2. Using tracing paper you can develop several design options using the same underlay (i.e., background / photo). (T/F)

3. With a digital camera it is possible to take several pictures (of a printed floor plan) and pick the best angle later. (T/F)

4. You need to use a computer in this chapter. (T/F)

5. A block of wood can be placed on the 2D floor plan before photographing it to suggest height. (T/F)

6. A 2D floor plan can quickly be put into _____ by taking a picture of it and printing it out.

7. Photographs provide perspective references which aid in adding new lines to the scene. (T/F)

8. Multiple sketches allow the designer to try many design options and ultimately find the best solution. (T/F)

Self-Exam Answers:
1 - T, 2 - T, 3 - T, 4 - F, 5 – Photo

~blank page~

Computer Model Underlay

*When contemplating a sketching method to use when one is about
to embark on a new design, there are a few factors to consider;
project budget and complexity, perceived number of design options,
and size. Sometimes doing everything by hand is the best route
given the project's small and non-complex size. Other times the
designer will benefit greatly from a hybrid approach which takes
advantage of both the computer and hand sketching – this chapter
will speak to the latter scenario.*

There is no "right" way in which to document one's design ideas during the commission of an architectural project; this should be made clear up front. However, one might utilize a process that takes so much time to draw that one is not able to develop the ideal design solution. Maybe the designer starts drawing lines in a computer program before ever sketching a few rough ideas on paper. Or maybe the designer spends an exorbitant amount of time sketching details into each design idea. In any case too much time is spent "spinning their wheels" and therefore not enough time is left to explore other options or to make needed changes.

As previously mentioned in this book, the reader will not actually be required to utilize any software to complete the exercises in this book. If you are using this textbook in a classroom setting, you may be asked to expand upon these exercises in various ways, including using software, by your instructor.

This chapter will introduce you to the process of generating a base model in the computer which allows for multiple views and quick changes. Several software programs exist in which you may model a mass object to trace over. As you will see in a moment, the software used in this discussion is Google *SketchUp*. Other programs exist like AutoCAD, Revit Architecture, 3DS Max, Rhino, Form Z, etc. One of the main reasons *SketchUp* is used here has to do with the program's ease of use and cost. The basic *SketchUp* program is free (http://sketchup.google.com/) and a professional version is offered for purchase.

Introduction

This perspective method utilizes a very simple form base generated by computer software which can be created very quickly. In this example Google ***SketchUp*** software was utilized to "mass up" or "block up" the building form; you can also add people and trees (entourage) all in about fifteen minutes. Dashed guidelines provide lines for sketching guidance. A quick rendering over this massing model is very accurate with regard to scale, and can be quickly drawn. This process combines the speed of both the computer and the artistic strokes of the hand, thus optimizing both. Adding much more detail to the *SketchUp* model requires more and more time (depending on how far you take it), which can often be done more quickly by hand.

Creating this accurate of a drawing base by hand would have taken much more time to do by hand than the 15 minutes taken using the computer.

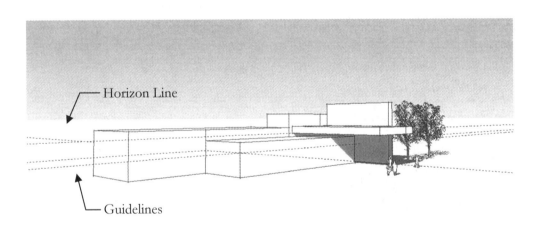

Base model created in Google SketchUp

Software can also very accurately depict the shade and shadows created by the building automatically. Depending on the specific software, you can also specify your longitude, latitude, and north direction in conjunction with a specific month and time of day to yield accurate results used to validate your design intent. (e.g., sustainable design initiatives).

Notice in the computer generated model, on the previous page, that the *Horizon Line* is represented by the change in background color between the ground and the sky. It is also apparent that the people and trees are casting shadows. It would be simple to locate the *Vanishing Points* and add additional elements or masses to the design if needed.

The sketch below takes advantage of the shadows delineated by the computer model. Take a moment to compare the two images. Windows, doors, walks and roads have been added using the "located" *Vanishing Points* so they are in the correct perspective. Finally, the windows have been mostly darkened in (which is how they usually look in reality) with some areas left blank to give the impression of reflection.

Sketch base on computer generated model

The computer generated model has the advantage of being able to change the view of the model. This means you only have to create the model once and from it you can generate several printouts from various vantage points; aerial, eye level, or worm's eye, for example. On the other hand, if you started laying out a perspective drawing using the *Casting Rays* method and then decided it was the wrong view angle you would have to start over – including setting up *Vanishing Points* and the *Horizon Line*.

Below is a slightly different view of the same model used in the previous example. As you can see, not only was the view angle changed but a completely new design concept was developed.

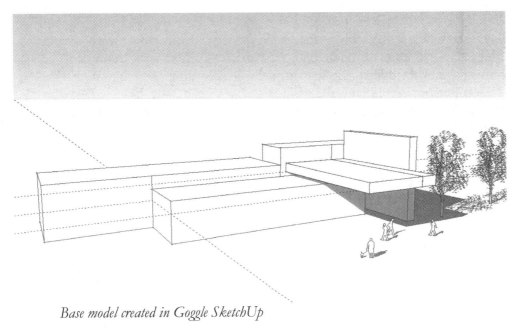

Base model created in Goggle SketchUp

Sketch base on computer generated model

French Language Village, LHB

An example of a more elaborate design is the **Place Plumereau** drawing for the *French Language Village* at Concordia Language Villages in Bemidji, Minnesota.

The very detailed and elaborate façade was first drawn in 2D as you can see in the image below. Then this design was turned into a very simple *SketchUp* base model. with numerous guidelines. Finally, an ink on vellum drawing was made over the printed *SketchUp* base drawing.

The detailed floor plans (first floor shown below) were drawn in Revit Architecture, which makes drawing accurate plans quick and provides real-time square footage (listed below each room number in this example).

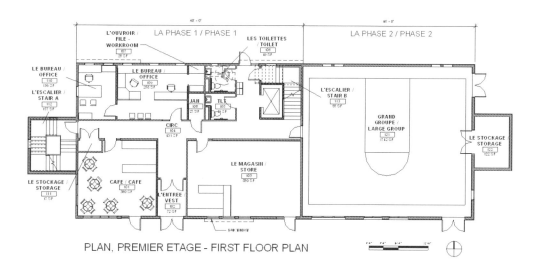

PLAN, PREMIER ETAGE - FIRST FLOOR PLAN

Exterior Elevation, drawn by Architect **Mark G. Poirier**

The image below is the base *SketchUp* model with shadows on and people added. Notice the many guidelines added for reference and the *Horizon Line*.

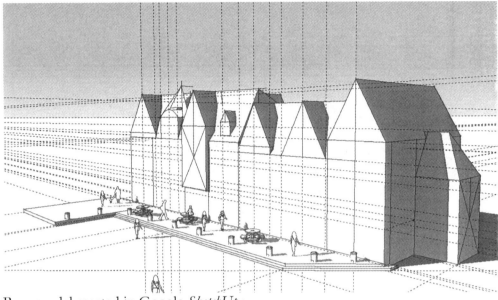

Base model created in Google *SketchUp*

Below is the "black & white" version of the sketch. This drawing would be more than adequate in many cases. However, the need occasionally arises in which the drawing needs to be rendered with color. This may be for public marketing or to "sell" the client on your design solution.

This next image, shown below, is an intermediate step between the previous image and the final rendered illustration. This is a copy of the sketch above, which has several color tests added and noted for reference. Once the preferred colors are found, the final drawing can be started on another copy. You should always use a copy (on bond) in case you mess up the colors; bond holds color better than tracing paper.

Many design firms have a large format printer with a scanner attached to it. (If the office does not have one you can usually find a business who provides this service.) This makes it easy to duplicate detailed sketches for colors and creating design options.

Large Format Scanner (left) and Plotter (right)

The final rendered image is clearly more interesting looking and explains the design intent more clearly. Notice the shadows match those derived from the *SketchUp* model previously shown.

Place Plumereau
Lac du Bois
LHB — FRENCH LANGUAGE VILLAGE
Perspective Extérieure
EXTERIOR PERSPECTIVE

CONCORDIA LANGUAGE VILLAGES
Concordia College, Moorhead, Minnesota USA

Images used by permission

The final image was scanned and composed in **Adobe *InDesign***, which is a page layout program used by graphic designers, where the banner was added across the bottom. A color print was made, which was about 24″x36″ in size and it was then attached to a foam core-board to present to the client; sometimes the design is only presented via a computer and digital projector in front of the client.

NAME_____DATE_____

Exercise 13-1

Computer Model underlay
This computer generated mass of a house should act as an accurate guide. Draw
over this guide and add windows, doors, siding/texture and entourage (people,
landscape, etc.). Utilize the shadows that the software has shown. You may want
to tear this page out and use it as an underlay if you have tracing paper; if not you
can sketch over this image.

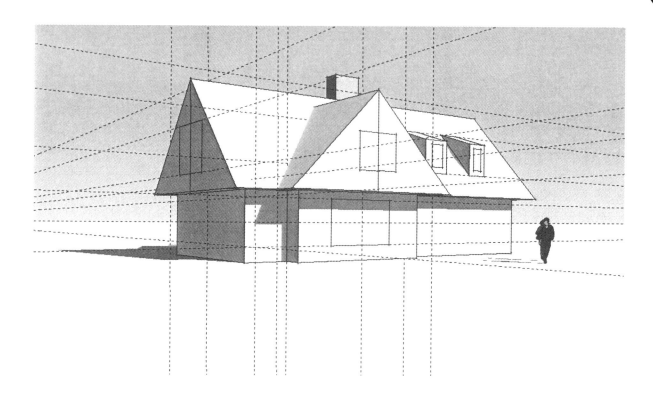

~blank page~

NAME_____DATE_____

Exercise 13-2

Computer Model underlay
Generate a sketch based on this computer generated image. **NOTE:** This is the same model used in the chapter discussion – just from a different angle.

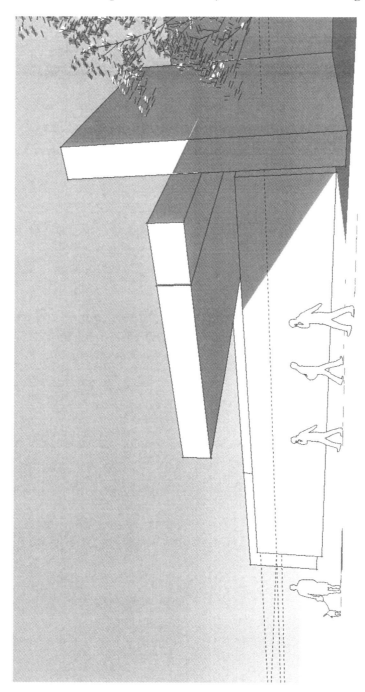

~blank page~

NAME_____DATE_____

Exercise 13-3

Computer Model underlay

This computer wireframe base with shade and shadow has been partially rendered-in using a felt tipped pen for the line work and a #2 pencil (or HB) for shade and some shadow lines over the felt tip lines. Complete the drawing, add trees in the background, siding texture, standing seam metal roofs, shrubbery and your own ideas of how the houses should look. Be inventive, but imitate the technique as much as possible, finishing with the pencil shading.

> NOTE: The image has been placed on the back side of this sheet to maximize its size.

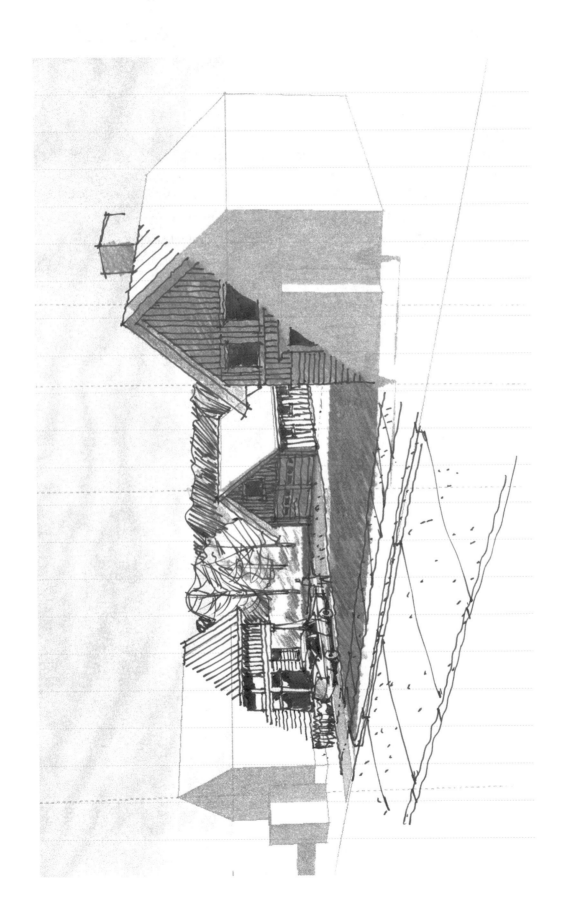

NAME_____ DATE_____

Self-Exam:
The following questions can be used as a way to check your knowledge of this lesson. The answers can be found at the lower left on this page.

1. Creating a 3D base model allows for several vantage points to be printed and used as an underlay. (T/F)

2. The *Entourage* do not cast shadows in the 3D software. (T/F)

3. Adding color to a rendering/sketch is typically optional. (T/F)

4. The DVD provides a video example of the computer model underlay technique. (T/F)

5. The software used reveals the *Horizon Line* (when it falls within the page). (T/F)

Review Questions:
The following questions may be assigned by your instructor as a way to assess your knowledge of this section. Your instructor has the answers to the review questions.

1. The software used in this chapter is costly. (T/F)

2. Although there is no "right" process for designing a building, if a method takes a ton of time it should be avoided. (T/F)

3. The 3D programs can add accurate *Entourage* and shadows. (T/F)

4. A basic model is created on the computer, which will be traced over, when utilizing the *Computer Model Underlay* method. (T/F)

5. It is often handy to create a test/reference copy of your rendering to explore marker colors. (T/F)

6. You will need to use computer software to complete the exercises in this chapter. (T/F)

7. A graphic design program like _____ can be used to combine a scan of a sketch with text/graphics for presentations.

8. The software used to create the base models in this chapter was Revit Architecture. (T/F)

Self-Exam Answers:
1 - T, 2 - F, 3 - T, 4 - T, 5 – T

Chapter 13 Questions

~blank page~

Section Four
A Real-World Project

The dialogue between client and architect is about as intimate as any conversation you can have, because when you're talking about building a house, you're talking about dreams.
Robert A. M. Stern

Architect David Salmela FAIA

The author's of this book would like to use this chapter to not only teach another valuable lesson on architectural drawing, but to also showcase the design process of an accomplished, award-winning, self-taught architect.

Award winning architect **David Salmela FAIA** utilizes the simplest methods to portray his architectural designs, believing that over-elaborate presentation methods consume precious funds that could be better put towards the design. His no nonsense method is as follows (which will be expounded upon on subsequent pages):

1). Pencil drawing on yellow tracing paper with red pencil poché (or hatch) for floor plans;

2). Pencil drafting of building elevations (2D drawings);

3). Photocopies of elevations are made using the "photograph" setting to best capture the subtleties of the pencil;

4). Using felt tipped pen to color windows black, and using pencil lines closely drawn in parallel fashion to render shadows and shade. Salmela creates a striking and understandable elevation image on the photocopier.

Salmela notes that if one presents a too finished and too complete an image to clients in the design phase, they often demonstrate disappointment simply because they get the impression that the design phase is done and they no longer can participate in the excitement of the design.

A journey through the process

Each designer's process for designing a building is unique but each invariably has several similarities. For example, most projects have a client, a budget, a site and a series of drawings that are presented to the client. Many designers, such as Salmela, start with a sketch book and generate numerous sketches exploring form and "drawing" out design solutions. These sketches, like the sample page shown below, are rarely shown to the client; rather they act as a springboard for ideas. Getting ideas on paper quickly is important in a process like architectural design which moves very quickly!

The image below is a page (approximately 4"x6") out of Salmela's sketch book. These sketches were drawn with pen and not burdened by the thought of presenting to the client – nor were they originally intended to be published here.

Check out the **Salmela | Architect** book

A book, written by *Thomas Fisher*, and photographed by *Peter Bastianelli-Kerze*, has been published featuring Salmela's work. You are encouraged to check it out for inspiration and more examples of 2D drawings plus models. The volume is SALMELA | ARCHITECT (University of Minnesota Press, 2005, ISBN-13: 978-0816642571). Also see his website: www.salmelaarchitect.com.

Below are a few additional samples from David Salmela's personal sketch books which he generously shared for inclusion in this textbook and for your growth! Hopefully these examples will help ease any anxiety you may have about the design process, as these beginning steps are not meant to be works of art.

The sketch pages below and the drafted views on the facing page illustrate the evolution of Salmela's design process, from sketches to clean and simple two-dimensional plans and elevations. Notice the windows are rendered with a solid black; this relates back to the discussion in the Entourage and Reflections chapter (Chapter 11) which mentioned glass gets darker near the ground and reflects the sky on higher stories of the building.

"Good architecture needs to resolve all programs for all users of a place with simplicity, beauty, and comfort." *David Salmela* (U of MN Press, 2005)

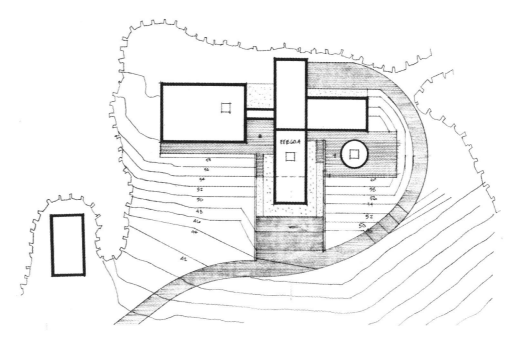

Site Plan

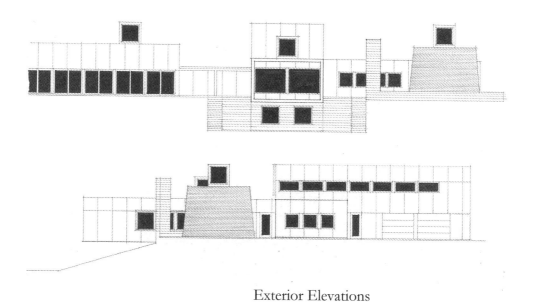

Exterior Elevations

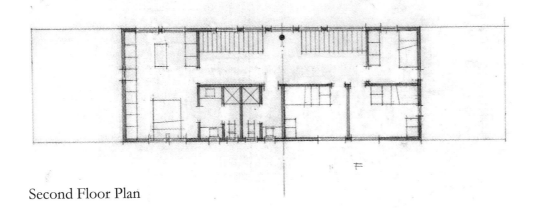

Second Floor Plan

First Floor Plan

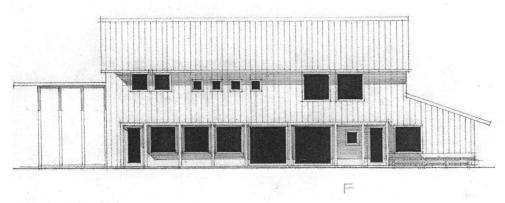

Exterior Elevation

These two facing pages provide yet another example of David's clean and simple drafting views. One elevation already has the windows blackened and shadows added to convey depth.

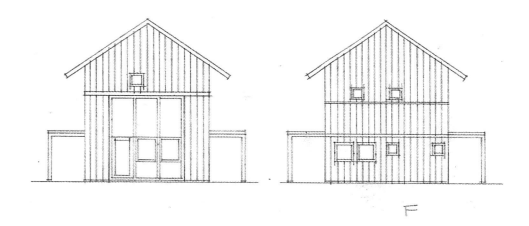

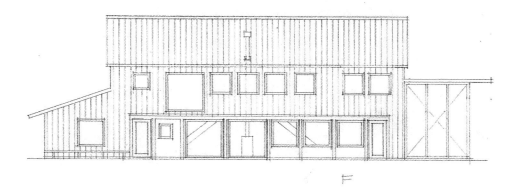

AIA, FAIA, CSI, LEED – what does this mean?

You may have noticed the alphabet soup (i.e., the letters) that follows many of the names mentioned in this textbook. These abbreviations are common in the professional world as they indicate various accomplishments; they actually serve as mini resumes in a way. Here is a quick break down:

AIA	member of the *American Institute of Architects* (aia.org)
FAIA	a Fellow in the AIA; candidates selected based on outstanding practice and service – a very prestigious designation
CSI	member of the *Construction Specification Institute* (csinet.org)
LEED AP	Leadership in Energy & Environmental Design (LEED) Accredited Professional (AP) – see usgbc.org for more info

Notes:

NAME_____ DATE_____

Exercise 14-1

Draft a Cabin Floor Plan
Produce a floor plan of a small cabin of your own design. Draw with pencil on tracing paper (or this page). Use a Red Pencil to Poché, or fill-in, the walls. Photocopy the results onto 8 ½″ x 11″ bond paper (**FYI**: Bond paper is just regular copy paper used in photocopy machines and printers). Remember to focus less on design and more on technique.

~blank page~

NAME_____ DATE_____

Exercise 14-2

Draft two Exterior Elevations

Develop two exterior elevations of your small cabin (from the previous exercise). Use pencil on tracing paper (or this page). Photocopy the elevations onto bond paper, color the windows black and use parallel pencil lines to create shade and shadow.

~blank page~

NAME_____ DATE_____

Exercise 14-3

Render Drafted Exterior Elevations
Photocopy the original, and then color the glass black (in both doors and windows) and use tightly spaced parallel lines to create shade and shadow. Finally, photocopy the results onto 8 ½" x 11" bond paper.

MᶜCOY HOUSE
1893

~blank page~

NAME_____DATE_____

Self-Exam:

The following questions can be used as a way to check your knowledge of this lesson. The answers can be found at the lower left on this page.

1. This chapter shows that 2D hand drawings can be very effective. (T/F)

2. Mr. Salmela often develops 2-point perspectives. (T/F)

3. David only shows one sketch per page in his sketch books. (T/F)

4. Shadows help convey _____ in 2D drawings.

5. All windows/glass are colored a solid _____ color.

Review Questions:

The following questions may be assigned by your instructor as a way to assess your knowledge of this section. Your instructor has the answers to the review questions.

1. It is believed, by Mr. Salmela, that over-elaborate presentation methods consume precious resources which are better used elsewhere. (T/F)

2. Drafted 2D plans and elevations are acceptable presentation drawings. (T/F)

3. What does LEED AP mean: _____

4. The _____ setting is used on the copier to best capture the subtleties of the pencil on paper.

5. What does AIA stand for: _____

Self-Exam Answers:
1 - T, **2** - F, **3** - F, **4** - Depth, **5** – Black

~blank page~

Index

S

T

V

W

Above: photo from one of the video shoots to create the instructional hand sketching videos which are found on the DVD that came with this book.

Video Index

Example of narrated video on sketching trees; located on the attached DVD.